EXTRA CASH FOR KIDS

Larry Belliston & Kurt Hanks

Wolgemuth & Hyatt, Publishers, Inc.
Brentwood, Tennessee

First published by Writer's Digest Books, Cincinnati, Ohio.

Wolgemuth & Hyatt, Publishers, Inc.
1749 Mallory Lane, Brentwood, Tennessee 37027.
Printed in the United States of America.

Library of Congress Cataloging-in-Publication Data

Belliston, Larry, 1949–
    Extra cash for kids.

    Reprint. Originally published: Cincinnati, Ohio : Writer's Digest Books, © 1982.
    Includes index.
    Summary: Discusses a variety of activities, such as yard care, crafts, garage sales, recycling, animal walking, junk removal, and house-to-house sales, which can be profitable as well as enjoyable.
    1. Money-making projects for children—Juvenile literature.   2. Self-employed—Juvenile literature.
    [1. Business enterprises.   2. Finance, Personal.
    3. Work.   4. Money]   I. Hanks, Kurt, 1947–   .
    II. Title.

ISBN 0-943497-70-1

Contents

Note to Parents

This book was written especially for kids. But we wanted to say just a word to the parents to let them know how helpful this book can be. Kids can read this page if they want to—but the action really starts on the *next* page!

Parents, you know and I know that it's a big, hard world out there when it comes to money. The last decade has brought home the pain of inflation and widespread unemployment. Adding to the problem is bad financial planning and the poor use of credit. Thousands of people have been caught in the credit-crunch, borrowing more than they can afford to, then spending their paychecks trying to keep up with the interest.

The younger generation is going to face a lot of the same problems—unless they learn sound financial practices. And the time to learn how to work, how to budget, and how to handle money, is when you're young. If you do, you'll establish life-long patterns and attitudes.

We all want lots of things out of life, and kids are no exception. But parents can no longer offer their kids a lot of extras. In fact, all too often it's hard enough just coming up with necessities. *Then* you have to worry about Alan's braces or Jenny's college, and suddenly it becomes a little overwhelming.

The answer, of course, is for the kids to get a job and earn part of their own way. But even that isn't as easy as it used to be. With labor regulations, minimum wage laws, increasing mechanization, and adult unemployment, the doors have closed on a lot of jobs kids have traditionally been able to get.

Extra Cash for Kids was written with these concerns in mind. The first thing it will do is help kids earn extra money *now*. The book has scores of suggestions—and descriptions—of how a kid can get onto his own payroll, whether he's eight or eighteen.

But this book won't just help them create jobs and then leave it at that. It teaches them the essentials of business management. It shows them how to keep records of their work. And it tells them how to make and follow a budget after the money is in hand.

While we talk about jobs and business skills in the book, we also try to reinforce the ideas of honesty, doing one's best,

1

caring about quality, giving a decent product for a fair price, and making others feel good. As kids learn the importance of such principles in the jobs they do, they'll be gaining an understanding of what it means to be a *good* worker. And, at the same time, they'll be learning the joy of work itself. The resulting attitudes will benefit your child throughout his entire life.

Most kids have lots of opportunities (in community, church, or school) to participate in different kinds of organized "enrichment activities." But few of those activities will be as satisfying as the old all-American idea of going out on your own and being an entrepreneur. By trying to make some money through their own efforts, kids will be able to implement their own ideas, learn through their mistakes, get the pride and satisfaction of personal accomplishment—and make some extra cash in the process. And that's a combination that can't be beat!

The Authors

Kids: Read This First!

If there's is one thing everyone needs a little more of, it's money! Clothes, food, transportation, movies, sports—you name it. If it's something you like or want, it probably costs. Even helping other people out or enjoying nature sometimes costs money.

And you probably need money too. That's why you're reading this book! As you flip through the pages, you'll find idea after idea for earning extra cash in your spare time. Each idea will tell you everything you need to know about that job. The only thing you'll need to add is experience—and you can pick that up on the job.

How do you decide which job will work best for you? The first thing to do is find out what kind of work the job involves. Will you be selling, or making something, or cleaning up, or what? What do you most enjoy doing? Do you think you'd like to talk to someone about buying Christmas cards, or would you rather change the oil in a car? Would you prefer to clean out a basement, or to make dried flower arrangements? The first and most important question you can ask in picking a job is: *What would I most enjoy doing?*

The second question is almost as important: *Can I make the money I need in doing that thing?* You might pick an idea that would be a lot of fun, but maybe it won't pay you enough to be worthwhile. Say you decide you'd like to provide a Halloween insurance service for your neighbors. That would be fun to do, but it's good for only about one week. Then you have to find something else.

Ideas might not make you enough money if:
they're seasonal, like Halloween insurance;
everyone else is doing the same thing;
no one wants to buy the product or service;
it takes too long to make or do.

The third question to ask when picking a job: *Do I have the necessary skills?* You'll have a hard time being a photographer if you don't know how to handle a camera. It's pretty difficult to sell dried flower arrangements if you haven't learned how to make them. But if you find a job you think you'd really like, but you don't know how to do it, don't despair—go on to the next question.

If I don't have the necessary skills for the job, am I willing to learn them? If we had to know everything in advance, we'd never get anywhere. Luckily, we can *learn*. And if you're willing to learn, you're in business.

But before you set up shop, you'll need to answer a few more questions:

Am I willing to give this job as much time as it will need?

If it takes money to get started, do I have enough? If I don't, am I willing to save, or find a partner or investor?

If the job is something that takes space, do I have enough?

If the job requires the help of my parents, do they have the time to do it?

If I need transportation to do the job, will I be able to get it?

Will I need to get a business license? (Check with your city or state officials.)

Will I need to be licensed by the state health department? (You may need to if you're working with food.)

Will I need to collect state sales tax when I sell things? (Check with state officials.)

Your answers to these questions will help you know what to do next. Chances are that you won't have to worry about licensing—your operation will probably be too small. And most of the ideas don't take much money to get started on, or much space, so you should be okay there too. But ask the questons. It's vital to know the answers before you start.

Picking a job is like buying a suit of clothes—you don't just grab the first thing that's handy. Instead you look at the sizes, think about colors, compare prices. Only after finding a style that you like—and only after you're sure you have a good fit—do you pay for the clothes and wear them to school.

It's not hard to find a suit of clothes you're satisfied with. And it's not hard to find a job that will be fun and help you get the extra cash you need. All you have to do is take a good look before you leap!

How This Book Works

After you've found a job you want to try, there's something else you'll need to keep in mind. When kids go to work, they often go into business for themselves. Maybe they'd like to work for someone else, but those kinds of jobs are often hard to come by. So they set up shop for themselves. Will they suceed? They probably will—if they've chosen the right job and if they're willing to be businesslike.

What's businesslike? It means a person is willing to keep records and figure profits. He's willing to keep track of how much money is coming in and how much is going out—and where it's going. He's willing to advertise. And give his customers a fair shake. He's willing to learn about providing extra services and packaging.

The person who does a good job with those things is ten steps ahead of the person who doesn't, no matter how old he is. To help you, we've included most everything you need to know about those things (and many others) under the heading **SuperIdea!**

By combining the information in the **SuperIdea!** sections with the ideas in the job sections, you'll have just what you need to get going. Good luck—and may your pockets be full of *extra cash!*

Yard Care

Mowing and trimming lawns and caring for gardens and the yard

Taking care of lawns is one of the oldest money-making tricks around. There's a reason why it's so popular: it really works! The job pays well and it's easy to find and do the work. And there are thousands of kids around the country who'll back us up when we say that a summer's earnings will easily last through the winter.

How to Do It

Find a customer. Start with your family, friends, and neighbors. If they don't give you enough work, ask them for *referrals*—names of other people you can check with. Another approach is to knock on the doors of older couples or those without kids of their own—these are the best bet for needing your help.

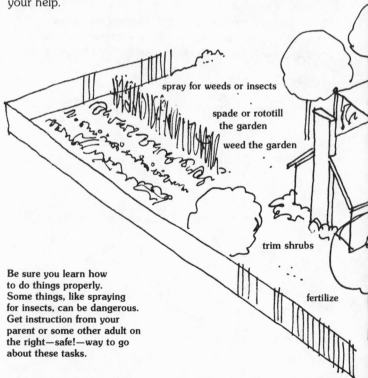

spray for weeds or insects

spade or rototill the garden

weed the garden

trim shrubs

fertilize

Be sure you learn how to do things properly. Some things, like spraying for insects, can be dangerous. Get instruction from your parent or some other adult on the right—safe!—way to go about these tasks.

Set a price.   If you don't know what to charge, ask around to find what things are going for. Each lawn will be different, and the amount of work each homeowner will want will be different. Set your price according to what you'll be doing. If you use your own equipment, you'll want to charge a little more. Make sure you and the homeowner agree on the price before you start. Also agree on *when* he'll pay—right after you do the work is best.

Set a schedule.   Get in the habit of doing your work according to a set schedule. Get your work done first and play later. It's much easier to stay ahead of things than to try to catch up when you're behind. Find out how often the homeowner wants you to come by, and then *do it*! (If you're rained out, talk to the owner to see what he wants you to do.

Understand the job.   Before you can do a top-notch job, you need to find out *exactly* what the homeowner wants done. Tell him (or her) you are willing to do most anything. Ask him to walk with you around the yard to look things over and explain exactly what he wants. Take notes.

Some of the things you might volunteer to do are:

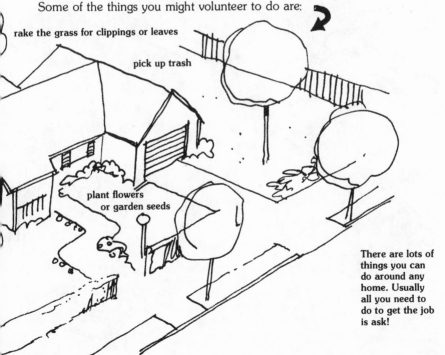

rake the grass for clippings or leaves

pick up trash

plant flowers or garden seeds

There are lots of things you can do around any home. Usually all you need to do to get the job is ask!

7

Special Notes

Know how to use the equipment. Before attempting any
lawn or garden jobs, ask your parents to show you how to use
the necessary equipment. You may already know this, but it
doesn't hurt to go over it once again for safety reasons.
Equipment you might be using includes:

lawn mower (gas, electric, or push)
edge trimmer
hedge trimmer
weed fork
grass shears
pruning shears
shovel
rake
rototiller
weed killer or insect spray bottle
fertilizer spreader

Learning how to
use equipment
properly can
save you a lot of
pain!

Getting other work.   One benefit of this kind of work is that it leads to other kinds of income. Some homeowners will want you to do other jobs, such as feed and walk the dog, help with special clean-up tasks, wash windows, and even watch their home and yard while they are on vacation. Or, your lawn job may turn into permanent work later on. The homeowner might hire you to work at his company or he might write a letter of recommendation when you go job hunting somewhere else.

Be sure you do a thorough job. It'll pay off.

MoneyMaker!

Selling Garden Seeds

Spring rolls around and a lot of people get the itch to go work in their gardens. So they pull out their tools, spade up the garden plot, and then go out to buy seeds. Some eager beavers buy their seeds even earlier!

If you're quick on the draw, you can sell them the seeds before they buy them elsewhere. Get a bunch of high-quality seeds from a seed distributor (that means don't buy the ten for $1 variety), and try to undersell the local merchants. Select seeds for plants that grow well in your area. (If you're unsure what grows well, ask a parent, neighbor, or local plant nursery worker.)

At the same time, you may want to sell flower seeds for people who enjoy splashes of color around their house all summer.

MoneyMaker!

Be a Tutor

If you have information other people would like to have, or if
you have a skill or expertise you could share, maybe you could
sell it by being a tutor. But you must know something well
enough to teach it to another person.

Here are some things you might teach:
- games—chess, checkers, video games, backgammon,
  billiards
- sports—basketball, baseball, football, tennis, racquetball,
  Ping-Pong, bowling
- martial arts—judo, karate, kung-fu
- singing
- dancing
- art
- musical instruments—guitar, drums, piano, recorder, violin,
  saxophone, and others
- the three Rs—reading, writing, 'rithmetic
- science
- penmanship
- foreign languages
- sewing

The key is to find something you know about that others
wished they knew about. And then to teach them.

To get started as a tutor, try one or all of these approaches:
- talk to your teacher or principal to see if they know of
  students who could benefit from your help
- talk to the community education people to see if they'll let
  you set up a class
- spread the word among your friends and ask them to spread
  the word farther
- distribute flyers in the areas where there are lots of kids
- put an ad in the area newspaper
- put a notice in your school newspaper

- put notices on the bulletin boards of Laundromats, supermarkets, and schools

Most of your tutoring will be done at home (either yours or the student's), and you'll probably tutor only one person at a time. Check with your teacher or principal to see how much tutors in your area charge.

MoneyMaker!

Raising Worms

Worms are easy to raise. All you need is a box or tub a couple of feet square filled with dirt about ten inches deep. In addition to the dirt, add manure, peat moss, and vegetable scraps (all kinds).

You can get the worms out of your own backyard, from a friend, or from a store that sells bait. Put them in your box and let them go. They'll lay eggs, and more eggs. In three months time, you'll have literally hundreds ready to sell. And they just keep on multiplying. The box will hold several thousand.

If you don't have enough worms to supply your customers, simply start another box of worms.

But before you start, make sure you have a place to sell them. Also make sure your parents approve of the idea, and that you have a place to keep worm boxes. You can sell your worms to fishermen, to sporting goods stores, and to gardeners who want to improve their soil. If one or all of those will use a good supply of worms, get going. They're easy to raise and almost as easy to catch!

Shoe-Shine Person

Taking a shoe-shine kit from door to door, or office to office, and shining people's shoes

Most people like their shoes to look clean, shiny, and well-groomed. But they often don't have time to keep their shoes shined.

If someone came to the door and offered to shine shoes for a reasonable price, many people would take him up on it in a minute. He'd be giving a valued service, one that many people can't get easily elsewhere.

How to Do It

Put together a kit. Start by making a shoe-shine kit. Buy a few basic kinds of polish. Buy colored as well as clear, for standard leather as well as patent-leather shoes. Paste polish is generally better than liquid.

Without a kit, you're just another kid on the street. But with a shoe-shine kit in hand, you can be a real professional!

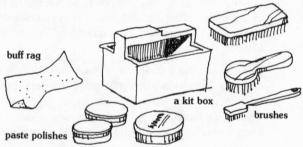

buff rag

a kit box

brushes

paste polishes

Buy some paste applicators. You can get cloths or little brushes for this purpose. The brushes usually work better.

Get some brushes to buff up the shoes, and some soft cloths to give them the final polish.

Learn how to shine shoes. If you can, find a shoe-shine stand in your area and go and just watch for a while. See how the shiner does his job.

Here are the basic steps to shining shoes:

1. Clean the shoe off, removing mud and dust.

2. Put the polish on with a little brush. Don't put it on too thick, just a thin layer over the part of the shoe you need to polish.

Don't get any polish on the bottom of the shoe. It will come off where it's least wanted, like on the customer's carpet.

3. Get out your polishing brush and rub with light strokes back and forth over the area you polished. The brush will take off the excess polish and put a shine on the shoe.

4. Get out the polishing cloth and give the shoe a final rub down.

Set a price.   When you visit the shoe-shine stand, make a note of how much the shiner is charging. You can charge a

Shoes with a fancy shine on them look twice as nice!

comparable price. But you're giving added service by going to the customers. Keep that in mind when you set your price. Also keep this in mind: if you can tell the customer you're cheaper than other local shoe shiners, you'll probably pick up more business.

It's not hard to find customers—just look for people with shoes on their feet!

Find customers.   Your customers are all over the place. All you have to do is let them know you're available.

Probably the best approach is to go from door to door with your kit. Tell people what you're up to and see if they'll let you shine their shoes on the spot. You can:

A. Shine them right on their feet. (Be sure to take some newspaper with you to protect the floor.)

B. Take them out onto their porch and shine them there.

C. If it's cold, take them home and deliver them later in the day. Be prepared by taking a sack with you. Be sure to check to see how long you can keep them.

Another place you might try is an office building. Get

permission from the office manager first. Then pull out your newspapers and go to work.

There are certain customers you should try to avoid: those with nurses' shoes, saddle shoes, and sneakers!

Set a schedule. Once you have a happy customer, keep him happy. The best way is to get on a regular schedule for shining the shoes. Agree to come back the last Saturday morning of the month, or every other Wednesday evening, or every Monday just after school.

A Success Story

With some kids, shoe shining is more than just a job—it's a rung on their ladder to success. A boy once set up a shoe-shine stand outside a bank. The bank people didn't mind, and it was a good place to meet customers.

One day the bank president came by. "I could use a shine," he said. "Can you do me a good job real quick?"

"You bet," the boy said enthusiastically. He got out his shoe-shining stuff and had the job done in nothing flat. The bank president was so pleased that he gave the boy a nice tip.

A week later, the president stopped again. "You did a great job, but with these feet of mine it just didn't last. How about another shine?"

The boy grinned and shined the shoes again—and got another tip.

The banker started to make it a habit after that. Every week he'd have the boy shine his shoes. And every week he'd offer a generous tip.

After working by the bank for a couple of years, the boy closed down his shoe-shine stand and went to work someplace else. But here's the neat part: years later the boy decided to make a career of banking. He went back to that same bank to see if they would offer him a job. The old bank president was still there—and he remembered his old shoe-shine boy.

"I know your work," the president said. "And I believe it would be to this bank's advantage to have a person like you working here."

When we do good work, people notice. And they're usually willing to let us work for them again.

MoneyMaker!

Selling Light Bulbs, Shoe Laces, and Other Necessities

Certain items are always in short supply. And you never have them when you need them most. For example:

- light bulbs
- shoe laces
- batteries (assorted sizes)
- scotch tape
- masking tape
- Elmer's-type glue
- epoxy glue

You get the idea. The list could go on and on. The idea is that people never seem to remember to buy these items at the store—and they always wish they had.

If you were to stop by their house with a good sales pitch, chances are you'd have some customers.

You can get your merchandise from local stores, or, if you're able to sell quite a bit, you might be able to get it from a wholesaler. Take the items with you in a day-pack or a bag when you go out to sell.

SuperIdea!

What Adults Think   A lot of your business will be with adults. If you know what they're thinking, it will be much easier to sell yourself to them. Some of what they think about kids is pretty positive. That's good to know, because you can reinforce their good thoughts by being just the kind of person they thought you were. And when they think bad things about kids, that's good to know about too—then you know what kinds of barriers you have to overcome.

Some of the negative things some adults think about kids:
- kids are messy (overcome by being super-neat)
- kids are to be seen and not heard (be super-polite)
- kids are noisy (be soft spoken and courteous)
- kids are obnoxious (never be pushy, and never know more than the adult—even if you really do!)
- kids are irresponsible (do your job better than an adult would)

Some of the positive things some adults think about kids:
- kids are cute (be cute, if you dare)
- kids are smart (know what you're up to, inside and out)
- kids are helpful (give them what they need)
- kids are little adults (be a true professional)
- kids are capable of doing good work (do even better than they expect)

The key in dealing with adults and their ideas is to overcome the negative and emphasize the positive. That's not as hard as it may sound. All you really have to do is be serious about your work, and let it show. When the adult sees that you really will be able to give him what he needs, any objections he may have about your age will vanish.

Selling Soft Drinks

Selling and delivering drinks to thirsty workers

People who are working hard can get pretty thirsty. And more often than not they've failed to bring enough water or other drink with them. So there they are, out there in the hot sun, sweating and straining, and they don't have anything to drink.

If some kid came up with some soft drinks they could buy, they'd welcome him with open arms! But first they'd buy his drinks. He could get some extra cash in a very short time.

How to Do It

Find a drink supplier. It's easy enough to go to the supermarket and buy some soft drinks to sell. But if you can find a wholesaler, you'll be able to get the drinks cheaper and end up with even more profit.

Give people what they want, and they'll be willing to pay what you want.

To find a soft drink distributor, look up *Beverages* in the Yellow Pages of the telephone book. Choose a couple of companies and call them, find out what their ordering procedure is. You'll have to buy the drinks by the case.

Set a price. It's best if you can stay competitive with the prices the supermarkets charge. But you can add to that and still make money. The workers will understand if your drinks cost more; after all, you're *delivering* it.

Find customers. Customers for cold drinks are fairly easy to find. Look for construction sites (but be sure not to go into places where you're not supposed to—most will be marked with a sign), road workers, and parks. If you get permission, you might also try factories and plants and the like. You'll hit the workers at the best time if you go during their coffee breaks. Be sure you take four or five dollars worth of change with you; many of your customers won't have the exact amount you need.

Here's an effective sales pitch you can try: "Excuse me, want to buy a cold drink?" That can develop to other pitches: "Cold pop for sale! Cold pop for sale!" The key is to be polite and at the same time make sure everyone knows what you have to offer. Don't fall into the trap of being too informal: "Hey, wanna pop?"

Take the drink right to the thirsty worker for the very best business.

Special Notes

Expand to other items.   Once your business gets going, you might want to expand to other items. Candy is always a big seller, especially if you pick favorites. Another good item might be sandwiches. Workers get hungry almost as much as they get thirsty, and the food is usually farther away than they want it to be. Get a name for showing up when they want, with the items they want, and you'll soon have a thriving business going for yourself.

One summer a kid in our neighborhood started selling pop to some men who were working construction in our area. He made extra cash at it—but then they turned it into something even better. They asked him to run errands for them. They were getting high wages, and were willing to pay him well for helping them out.

Berry Starts

Growing and selling raspberry or strawberry starts

Raspberry and strawberry plants like to spread all over creation—they send out runners under the ground and start new plants right next to the parent plants. If they aren't thinned out every year, the whole patch will grow unsightly. The plants will get too crowded and won't produce properly.

The thinning process solves the problem. It also brings a benefit: those new plants that have been pulled out can be planted somewhere else. They can even be sold for money!

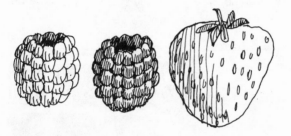

There's nothing people love more than berries—of all kinds!

How to Do It

Get the starts. The starts are really the roots, or the parts that have been pulled out of the ground. They're called starts because they are the start, or beginning, of a brand-new plant.

There are three places where you can get starts to sell:

1. Grow your own plants. Find a plot of ground where you can put them and plant them early in the fall. By spring they'll be ready to thin, and you'll be ready to sell some. The next year you'll have even more.

2. Find a neighbor who raises berries. Offer to thin his berries for free—all you want is to be able to keep the starts. You'll both benefit.

3. If you don't have a place to grow your own berries, and you don't have any neighbors who have some, you can still buy some from a wholesale or bulk nursery. They'll want you to buy in quantities—but you'll almost certainly be able to get rid of all you buy.

When you want to thin the plants, here's how you do it: First, you'll be able to see where the start is sticking out. With the strawberry it will look like a little green plant. With the raspberry it will be more like a cane. Dig around every plant, until you can pull it out with the roots. Then stick the start in a paper cup, or wrap it in a wet newspaper. Be sure the roots don't get dry. If they do, your plant will die.

The best time to thin is in the spring, right when you're ready to sell the plants.

Set a price. Before you go out selling, you need to decide on how much to charge. The best way to do this is to check around at local nurseries and greenhouses and other stores that are selling plants and find out what they charge. Set your price so it's competitive—hopefully a bit less than everyone else is charging.

Toward the end of winter, people start to get the heebie-jeebies—they want to get out into their gardens, out of the house. As soon as spring breaks, they'll be ready for your product of berry starts.

Find customers. Two approaches will work here. You can post notices on community bulletin boards. That will probably bring you some orders. But don't wait around for the calls to come in. Go out and try the other approach.

The best time to try to sell your starts is in the early spring. When it starts to warm up and people begin to work out in their yards, they'll be pretty interested in buying new plants. Get them at the right time and you'll have as much business as you can handle.

Find a neighborhood where the people obviously care about their yards and go door to door selling your starts. It will help if you can have the starts right there with you, in a wagon or a box. If you can't, be sure you return quickly to fill the orders you've received.

Special Notes

Plant the starts for an extra charge. Some of the people you talk to may want the berry plants but will want some help in planting them. You can volunteer to do that for a small extra charge. That will help you sell more plants and earn additional money as well.

Doing that kind of service can open other doors, too. If you show the people that you can do a good job with the berries, they might be more willing to let you come back and help them with other garden or yard work. One job can lead to another. If you're dependable, you might be able to find yourself enough work to keep you busy all summer.

Try herb starts. If berries work well, you might also decide to try herbs. Plants like chives, parsley, and sage are fun to have around, and they propagate themselves the same way that berries do. You can easily expand your business into other kinds of plants. Once you get a name for yourself, you'll be able to work in your business every summer, selling more and more as your own plants get more and more mature. Some plants are tricky to grow, though, so learn what you're doing in advance. The library will have some books that will tell you just what you need to know.

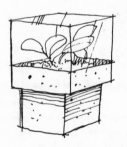

At the same time as you're selling berry starts, you can sell herb plants too.

SuperIdea!

Use Smart Packaging Packaging is an important part of any business. *Packaging* simply refers to the kind of container or cover or wrapping you put your product in. If you put the product in a nice package, you'll be more likely to sell it. If the package is crummy, or it there isn't a package at all, you'll have a harder time.

You've probably heard of the Pet Rock. That was an example of packaging genius. The product was an ordinary rock. But the package turned it into something more—a pet! The package gave instructions on the care and feeding of the pet rock. It made the rock attractive as a gift. And it made its developer a millionaire overnight.

Not too long ago a company in Milwaukee was trying to sell human waste as fertilizer. Now, human waste makes good fertilizer, but no one was overly excited about buying it. So the company called it Milorganite, and put it into an attractive package. Suddenly people were willing to buy it.

It didn't matter that the product was exactly the same. It didn't matter that its value hadn't increased one bit. What did matter is that the package was attractive, the name of the product was attractive. And that made people want it.

What about when Mount St. Helens blew her top? Hundreds of miles of land were covered with ash from the volcano—worthless, dirty, disgusting ash. Then someone put it into a nice package and marked $3.95 on it. And that one simple act made that worthless ash worth something.

Whatever you're trying to sell, put it into a nice package. Give it an inviting name. Make it *look* like something people would want to buy. And then they will.

Rent-a-Kid

Renting out your services to people who need them

People in every city have odd jobs that they aren't too excited about doing. And kids in every city are willing to do those kinds of jobs for a little pocket money.

That's how Rent-a-Kid was born. Some enterprising soul decided to match the people with jobs with the kids who were willing to do them.

You can do the same thing in your area. You can seek out jobs for yourself, or, if business booms, you can set up a whole company of Rent-a-Kids!

How to Do It

Offer a variety of services.   The more services you offer, the better your chance of getting customers when you advertise. Consider the following:

A little advertising will go a long way.

window washing
cleaning rugs
cleaning fireplaces
cleaning gutters
cleaning basements
   and attics and garages
cleaning swimming pools
dog washing
recreational vehicle
   and boat washing
car washing
grocery delivery

errand running
babysitting
home watching
animal walking
party helper
lawn mowing
raking leaves
garden tending
house painting
hauling junk away
shining shoes
doing dishes
vacuuming floors

Set a price. Most of what you do, you'll do by the hour. Decide on an hourly rate before you even start. Check around with other kids in the area to see what they're getting for those kinds of jobs—or ones like them.

Make your price competitive, then mention it in your advertising. People are more likely to call if they know exactly what you'll be charging them. If you don't say anything about charges, they'll assume that you'll cost more than they want to spend.

Find customers. There are four ways to get customers for a Rent-a-Kid business. You might try a combination of all four:

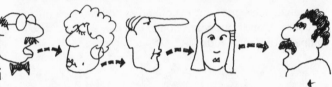

The best way to get customers is word-of-mouth recommendations. Do good work and you'll get all kinds of referrals.

1. Word of Mouth. Ask your parents and their friends to spread the word that you're available. Whenever you do a job for someone, ask them to recommend you to others, if they were pleased with your work. (Make sure they're pleased!)

2. Flyers. Make up a leaflet and pass it around from door to door. Explain just what kinds of services you can provide, and how much you charge.

3. Posters and notices. Hang ads up on community, grocery store, and Laundromat bulletin boards.

4. Classified ads. Put an ad in the paper, but don't make it too long, or it will cost too much. Your ad might look like this:

> Too much to do and not enough time? Call Rent-a-Kid! Can mow lawns, babysit, clean attics, walk dogs—and much more! Call Tom at 363-7892.

Set a schedule.   Once you have a customer you've agreed to help, see if they'll put you on a schedule. That means you'll be able to go to their house or apartment at the same time every week (or every day) to perform your Rent-a-Kid services.

The schedule will make a lot of difference to the profitability of your business. You won't have to sit around waiting for a customer to call, and you won't have to go beat the bushes for more work. You'll know that at 6 p.m. every Thursday you'll be at the Smiths mowing their lawn. Get that kind of schedule for every night you want to work, if you can.

Special Notes

Hire other kids.   When your business starts to grow (and it will), round up a bunch of other kids to help you. Choose kids that you know are reliable—or get recommendations from other kids. Change your advertising to indicate that Rent-a-Kid is a group of kids, not just one. Then, when a call comes in for services, match the kid with the job. Charge each kid on your list 10 percent or so for each job you get him. And make sure everyone on your list does an outstanding job—even an occasional bad job by your kids will give your business a bad name.

The Success of KIDCO, Inc.

Perhaps some kids will read about Rent-a-Kid and wonder if they can pull off that kind of business. It's true that it does take some work—and some guts. It's not particularly easy to pull together a group of kids into a working business—although it's not that hard, either, once you decide to make a go of it.

Once you put your mind to it, you can probably succeed at just about anything. But that means you have to be willing to pay the price of hard work to get the success.

Not too long ago, some kids in California actually got rich through some creative thinking and hard work. They noticed that people in their area needed fertilizer for their lawns and gardens. And they noticed that the people weren't getting it. They put their heads together and decided that they ought to be in the manure business--packaging and selling manure for fertilizer!

With some help from their parents, they learned what was needed in packaging fertilizer. Then they contacted some local dairy farmers to see if they could have some of their spare manure. The farmers were happy to let the kids clean up for them. So the kids put the manure in bags, processed it in a special way they'd learned, and sold it around the neighborhood.

It wasn't all easy. For a while they were putting in a lot of time and not getting much in return. But gradually the business grew. More and more people came to them for fertilizer. Before the kids knew it they were rolling in money from their manure!

That's when they decided to get even smarter. "We can't have all this money just sitting in the bank," they said. "We've got to do something with it." And they formed a corporation called KIDCO, Inc., to take care of their business and the money it made. They started to buy some real estate. They bought some more. Before they knew it, they had bought a whole town, complete with lodge, grocery store, and service station. They were worth hundreds of thousands of dollars now—and the money was still coming in from their business.

These kids were smart—but no smarter than most kids. These kids were willing to work hard—but no more than most kids. The key was that they made up their minds to make their business work. And they did what was necessary to make it happen.

SuperIdea!

Finding an Investor   Sometimes you'll have some fantastic ideas about how to make money—but you need a bit of money to get started. Even if you don't have a cent, don't give up. All you need is an *investor*. An investor will give you some of his money to get going, then you'll pay him back later, with a little extra for profit.

Where can you find an investor? Try these places:
- Dad or Mom
- Uncle or Aunt
- Yourself—save your allowance for a while
- Grandma or Pa
- Neighbors—get your parent's permission before you ask anyone
- A group of kids pitching in together, pooling their own money

When you ask for investment money, be businesslike about it. Know exactly how much you need, and explain exactly what you're going to do with it. For example, if you want to put together dried flower arrangements to sell for Mother's Day, find out how much the supplies will cost. Then go to your investor and say, "I need $35 to get going on the project."

Tell the investor when you think you can pay the money back—and tell him how much profit you think he'll make. Agree on a percentage: Maybe you'll give him 10 percent profit (an *extra* ten cents back for every dollar he gave you), or maybe 5 percent (an extra five cents back).

Once you have the investment money, guard it very carefully. Be sure to spend it only on your business. Keep good records, so you'll be able to show your investor just where his money went.

Then take care to pay him back on time. That will make him more willing to work with you on your next project. If for some reason you can't pay on time, don't just avoid him because you're worried or embarrassed. Talk to him and explain the problem, and tell him when you think you'll be able to pay.

Car Wash

People can go down to the car wash, put in a handful of quarters, and get a clean car for a dollar or so. But if it's a cold day, it's a miserable job. And if the day is nice, they have to wait in line forever. Sometimes it's just easier to drive a dirty car.

And then there's the interior—after they use the car wash, they still have to worry about cleaning the inside. It's all a pain in the neck for some car owners. They wish their car were clean, but it's hardly worth the hassle to dust the dash, wash the floor mats, and vacuum the crumbs from yesterday's oatmeal cookies.

Then you come to the door. You offer to wash their car for a couple of bucks, which is just about what they'd have to pay at the car wash—and you're bringing the job to them. You'll clean the interior for another dollar. Some people won't be interested—they'd rather have a dirty car. And some will think you're an angel from heaven.

Take your own hose, in case their lawn is watered by a sprinkler system and they don't have one. Also take rags, bucket, sponges, towels, window washer, squeegee, and, if you can, a friend! If you can take a portable vacuum, your work will go even more smoothly.

Addressing Envelopes

Some businesses send out monthly mailings to their customers. And it's a real headache for them—they have to put a couple of their secretaries to work for a couple of days to address and stuff all the envelopes. The work piles up—and still the secretaries are stuffing.

Check around with the businesses in your area to see if any of them send out periodic mailings. If they do, offer to do the envelope addressing and stuffing for them. You'll have to write or type the address on the envelope, then fold up the letter and stick it inside. They may also want you to attach a stamp.

Sometimes businesses also need labels stuck on envelopes, and that's another service you could offer to perform.

Furnace Filters

Selling and delivering filters in the fall

It's not uncommon for people to go all through the winter without replacing their furnace filters. It isn't that they don't want clean filters—filters make the furnace run more cheaply and efficiently, and they'd be crazy not to want that. It's not that filters are too expensive—you can get a set for a couple of bucks.

Furnace filters help keep both the house and the furnace cleaner. They function by drawing the dirty air in on one side . . .

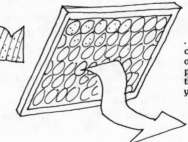

. . . and send out clean air on the other side. Some people change their filters twice a year.

The problem is that the person just keeps forgetting. When they're in the store, they remember: "Oh, yeah, I need to buy new filters." But they're not sure which is the correct size. Then when they get home they forget again, and it never gets done.

Someone would be doing them a real favor if they'd stop by their house and bring them just the right filters. It would be like the fairy godmother!

And that's just what this job is all about: taking filters to people's houses.

How to Do It

Plan early. The first cold spell comes and people start thinking about their furnaces. They stoke up the fire and bundle up for a long winter. That's the ideal time to sell filters. They know it's time to replace the filters in their furnaces, but they haven't done it yet. The earlier you can start, as long as it's at least chilly outside, the more filters you'll be able to sell.

Find a distributor. If you have to buy filters from the store and then resell them to the customer, you'll probably be able to make money. But you'll make even more if you can find a wholesale distributor. And you might even be able to beat the price of the regular store. How do you find a distributor? The best way is to look up in the Yellow Pages under *Hardware— Wholesale and Manufacturers.* Explain that you're a new retailer and will be buying in bulk. Find out their prices for different size filters.

Set a price. After you know what the wholesale people sell their filters for, check around at some of the retail stores. That will give you some idea of how much you can charge. If you want to charge more than the retail stores do (especially if you end up buying from them), you'll still do a good business. But if you can sell for a bit less, you'll do even better.

Take orders. This is a job that calls for door-to-door sales. Start by going around your neighborhood (unless you live in an apartment) and tell the people what you're doing. Explain that you'll deliver the filters they need for such-and-such a price. Tell them how soon they can expect you to bring the filters by. *Make sure you find out what size filters they need, and how many.*

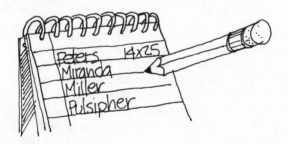

Keep a list of people you sell filters to, as well as the size their furnace takes. That will make it easier to sell to them next year.

Buy and deliver the filters. After you have a batch of orders, you can go buy the filters. Handle them carefully; filters are not made for rough treatment and can easily break. You can collect your money as you deliver. If the people don't have the money right then (although they almost certainly will, since we're talking about only a couple of bucks), don't leave the filter. Tell them you'll bring it by another day.

After you've made all your deliveries, keep a list of the people you sold to. They'll be good prospects for the next year.

31

MoneyMaker!

Showing Movies

In these days of the video explosion, it's getting easier and easier to show enjoyable movies at home. And that opens a door for you to make some money.

Start by passing out a flyer to all the homes with kids in your area. Tell them that you're having a "movie morning" at your house on Saturday. (If you don't have a big basement with a TV in it, you may need to find a partner). Cost can be $1 per kid—popcorn and punch can cost extra. Mention that it's a chance for the kids to have a good time—while mom and dad relax.

Once you feel you're going to have a good turnout, go to the local video rental shop and rent a video tape player, along with a couple of fun kids' movies. You'll probably have to let your mom or dad rent the stuff for you—most places won't give their stuff out to kids under 18. And a parent should probably be handy to supervise its use.

On the day of the movies, make sure you have lots of popcorn and punch for the kids. You'll probably make as much from those as you will from the movie. Charge 25 cents or 35 cents per bag (small bag) for the popcorn and 10 cents or 15 cents per cup for the punch. Don't be surprised if someone spills on the floor—in fact, you might as well expect it. But cleaning up behind them will all be worth it when you count your money at the end of the morning.

If the day is successful, you might want to make it a tradition, so kids and parents alike can come to expect that there will be a fun movie "over at the Anderson's" on the first Saturday of every month.

American Flags

Selling flags to homeowners for holiday display

A lot of people like to display American flags during national holidays: Presidents' Day, Memorial Day, Fourth of July, Labor Day, and Veterans's Day. And a lot more *would* do it, if only they had a flag. The problem is that they don't know where to buy one—or they forget about it until the holiday is already there and the neighbors are putting their flag out. Then it's too late.

Flags are a patriotic item, and a kid who sold them to interested people would be doing them a real favor.

Selling flags is a great project for clubs and groups. It's a natural for Boy and Girl Scouts.

How to Do It

Find a flag supplier. School supply stores will have flags in stock. And they can order more for you. Some variety stores also have them.

But an even better place is *their* supplier. Check under *Flags* in the Yellow Pages of the phone book and you'll find what you need. Get a catalog from the supplier, if you can, and maybe buy a sample or two. The supplier will help you know how much to charge your customers—probably 30 to 40 percent more than you pay yourself.

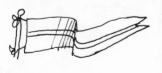

School flags, group flags, or even flags made for special occasions may also sell well.

Find customers.   The best way to sell your flags is to go door to door. Start in your own neighborhood and work out into other areas. Here's the kind of sales pitch you might try:

"Hello, I'm Henry Hansen. I live just down the block from you. I've noticed how nice some of the homes in this area look with flags hanging from them on holidays. It's fun to drive through an area like this and see logs of flags hanging. I'm selling American Flags today; I can get them cheaper than you can get them at the store, and I deliver besides!

"These pictures in the book will show you the different flags you can choose from. I've written the prices right beside them. Could I take an order for one of these smaller ones here, or do you think a bigger one would be better?"

Once the people have agreed to buy a flag be sure to get their money—before you order from the supplier. Once they've given you their money, though, you need to give them something: a receipt, and a promised date of delivery.

While you're selling flags, you can also sell flag accessories. Many flag purchasers will need poles to stand their flag on. Or they may need brackets to hang the flag from. Some people who already have flags may also be interested in these items.

If you decide to sell the American flag, be sure to show proper respect for it. (See the Boy or Girl Scout handbook for details on proper handling.)

Make deliveries.   Be sure to get your orders in early. If you don't you might miss the upcoming holiday. Once you get the flags in from your supplier get them out to your customers as fast as you can. They'll appreciate your promptness. And they'll remember when you try to sell them something next time.

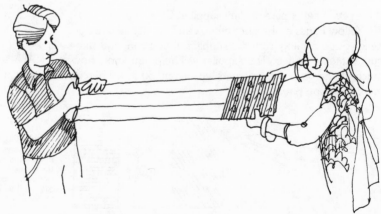

Cleaning Boats, RVs, and Airplanes

Find people with dirty vehicles and get paid for cleaning them up

Go out by the freeway some holiday and count how many boats and recreational vehicles (RVs) are going by. Or, if you are near an airport, see how many private planes there are. The numbers will surprise you: there are millions upon millions of such vehicles out there. And they're just waiting for someone to come along and clean them up.

Adults love to take a ride in their private planes. And hopping into the RV or skimming the water in a boat can be the highlight of the month. But someone has to clean up the mess when the playing's done. But sometimes adults don't have the time or energy to spruce up their toys.

The answer: you can do it for them.

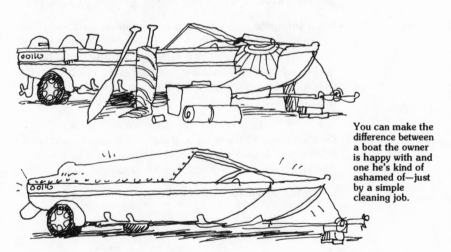

You can make the difference between a boat the owner is happy with and one he's kind of ashamed of—just by a simple cleaning job.

How to Do It

Find customers. Do some checking around. You might have quite a few boats and RVs in your neighborhood. You might know several people who own their own planes. Or you might have to go several blocks across town to find the people.

They're easy enough to find. A quick trip around town will tell you exactly where the boats and RVs are. And the owners of those will often be the same people who own planes.

Once you've found what you're looking for, line up your job. Approach the owner and tell him that you'll clean his boat, inside and out. He'll be prouder of what he owns, and will enjoy it more if it's clean. And you'll save him a good deal of time by doing the cleaning for him.

Another approach is to put flyers up in appropriate places: airplane terminals and hangars, boat and RV dealerships, and boat launching docks. Your flyer should include the services you'll perform and your name and phone number.

Set a price. After you've cleaned a couple of RVs or cleaned and waxed a couple of airplanes, you'll know better how much to charge. The key is to learn to predict how much time a particular job will take, and to decide how much per hour you want to make. With those two pieces of information, you'll be able to tell the customer how much the work will cost him. Be sure you have a firm agreement before you start. If you have to buy the supplies, include that cost in the price you charge.

Set a schedule. It's best if you can get on a cleaning schedule, instead of trying to line up new jobs all the time. Clean the same vehicles periodically. That way you'll be dealing with people you know and trust, and you'll be working with a vehicle you're more familiar with. The result will be a quicker, more efficient job.

Talk to the vehicle owner and ask when he'll be taking vacations with his RV or his boat. Arrange to clean them before or after that date—or both. Find out when the airplane owner flies his plane. Get on a schedule of cleaning it.

Learn the best way to clean and wax.

It's not hard to find out the best ways to clean: read the label on the package, talk to someone who's had experience, or read up on it in the library.

Special Notes

Start early in the season.   The sooner you can get with your customer, the more money you can make. And the better edge you'll have on your competition. If you put things off too long, you may end up without a job at all. But if you line up jobs before the season starts, you should be able to keep yourself busy. Boats are pretty much fair-weather items. But don't fall into the trap of thinking that people use RVs or planes only when the weather's nice. They can be used year-round—and they need to be cleaned year-round, too.

Learn special precautions.   The items we've been talking about are very expensive, and you could find yourself with a very unhappy customer if somehow you damaged something through carelessness. To avoid potential problems, make sure you understand any precautions you must take. If the owner of a plane wants you to clean the interior, for example, find out what things you *must not* touch. If you're going to clean the RV's carpet, make sure the carpet cleaner won't ruin the color. A little precaution goes a long way.

If you don't know how to clean something, don't hesitate to ask. The owner will only have to show you once (hopefully!), and you'll be able to clean without supervision many times after that.

Expand to other items.   Once you've established yourself as a reliable worker on one thing, you can probably expand to other things with the same customer. For example, you might be able to wash and wax his car periodically. Maybe he'll hire you to clean out his garage. And, if you do a good job, he'll certainly recommend you to his friends, who have boats, RVs, and planes to clean!

Boats, planes, and RVs are points of pride with their owners. Tell the owner, sincerely, how much you admire his vehicle. That will make him more willing to let you work on it.

MoneyMaker!

Sell This Book

The way to make it in any business is to find something that people want. For example, they may want help cleaning their house. If you can offer that help, you've got a job.

Maybe people want a nice centerpiece for their dining room table, and they haven't got one. So you make one and sell it to them.

Maybe someone wants Christmas wrap (everyone wants Christmas wrap!) in mid-December. If you can provide them with Christmas wrap, you'll have yourself a good business.

Now here's an idea you may not have thought of: one thing that kids want is a good way to make money. They don't have a job and they'd like to do something part time to give them the cash they need.

You can build a business by meeting that need. The approach? Buy a bunch of copies of this book and sell them to your friends. You're probably pretty familiar with it by now; you know what's in it. You can get excited when you describe it to your friends—you can tell them how it will help them, how it will meet their needs. Remember, that's the key to a good business: meeting the needs of people.

Once you've sold the book to your friends, you can sell it to other people. Put an ad in the school newspaper: "Great new book that will help you make the money you need! Call Jeff at 433-9292."

Put a poster on the school bulletin board: "101 failsafe ways to make the money you need! Learn them in EXTRA CASH FOR KIDS! Call Joni at 502-7601."

Or go door-to-door in areas where you know there are a lot of kids. Leave flyers on the doorstep, or talk to the *parents*.

Make a profit by adding a dollar onto the coverprice of each book. Or, better yet, see if you can get a local bookstore to cooperate with you. Have them provide the books to you, and then you take a percentage of each book you sell.

Change Car Oil

To be able to do this job, you'll need to know something about cars and the tools of the job. Even more important is the experience of having done it a time or two. To get the experience, ask your parents or a neighbor if you can change the oil in the car, under their direction. It's not a difficult job, and you'll be able to pick it up quickly.

It's crucial that you have the right tools. Nothing's more frustrating than trying to work on a car with tools that won't cooperate. You'll need a good socket wrench set, to get off stubborn bolts on oil pans; an oil-filter wrench; and a drip-pan to put the oil in. Take care to keep the oil in the drip-pan so it doesn't make a mess. (If it bothers you to get dirty, you should probably forget this job! No matter how careful you are, dirt and oil will almost certainly end up on you, somewhere. Wear old clothes.)

While you're changing the oil, you should also replace the oil filter. That usually requires some strength. You'll learn if you have enough when you do your first cars at home.

The best way to get customers for this job is to go door to door on a Saturday, and then do the jobs on the same day. In most places people can get their oil changed for $10 or $15, which includes the oil and oil filter. You may be able to charge that much, since you're taking the service to them—but you certainly shouldn't try to charge more. You should try to supply the oil and filter for the customer, which means you'll need to find out what make and year his car is (so you can get the right filter) and what oil he prefers (if he has a preference), then buy the materials, and then do the work. The customer may be willing to give you the money to buy the supplies before you do the work.

If you want to expand your service, you can learn how to change the water and anti-freeze in the radiator. That's an important job that's too often neglected.

Bird Feeders

Making bird feeders and selling them to people in your area

It's fun to watch hummingbirds. Their wings flutter so fast sometimes you can't even see them, and they flit from one place to another in the blink of an eye.

Lots of people would like to have hummingbirds or bluejays or woodpeckers on their property, but they rarely see them. One reason might be that they haven't tempted the birds to come by putting out a bird feeder. You could make those feeders and sell them for some extra cash.

How to Do It

Make a sample feeder. Before the customer will want to buy a feeder from you, he or she will want to know what it looks like. That means you need to make a feeder to show them.

There are a lot of ways to make an attractive bird feeder. Here's one you could make out of a milk carton. It won't sell for as high a price, but still it works, and it's pretty easy to make. (If you end up selling these, get empty cartons from your folks and from neighbors.)

Study up on the kinds of birds in your area, so you can talk intelligently with the people you sell feeders to.

You can also make a feeder out of wood. It's a little more complicated than a carton feeder, but customers will like it more because they'll know it will last longer. Other feeders can be made out of wire. Your library will have some books that will explain how to make all kinds of feeders.

Set a price. The price you set can include more than just the feeder. You can give the customer other things at the same time—and that will help you to make a little more profit.

Along with the feeder, you can provide:
- the first week's worth of seed
- an instruction sheet about the kinds of birds to watch for in your area (you can get information for this from your library or local Audubon Society—or you may want to sell paperback regional bird guides)
- information on where and how to hang the feeder

A good kind of hummingbird feeder can be purchased at discount stores. When they're filled with sugar water, they give great results.

After you've decided what you'll include with your feeder, you'll have an idea of how much you can charge. If you're giving the three things we just mentioned, you can probably charge a couple of dollars for the carton feeder and a couple more for the wooden feeder.

Find customers. Bird feeders work almost anywhere. You can sell them to people in houses, and you can sell to people in apartments. Almost everyone has a window they could hang a feeder out of, or a tree to hang it on.

It's probably best to start in your own neighborhood. Try to hang out your own feeder for a few weeks before you start selling—that way you can tell the customer how well it's working for you: "And I live only three blocks from here!"

Go from door to door and show the customer your sample bird feeder. Explain that you'll also provide instructions on hanging it and information on the kinds of birds that might come. You'll also give them the first week's worth of seed.

Your excitement about the idea will definitely help as you try to sell it. People like to feel excited. When they see that the bird feeder gets you excited, they'll want to buy one so they can be excited too.

When your customer agrees to buy, take down his name and address and tell him about how long it will be before you'll deliver the feeder. Ask for a dollar or two in deposit, so that the customer doesn't change his mind. Be sure to mark down the amount of the deposit before you leave, and give the customer a receipt.

Deliver the feeders. After you have the orders, you'll need to make the feeders, of course. And you'll need to put together your instruction and information sheets to hand out. It would probably be easiest just to make one copy of each and then to photocopy (Xerox) off as many copies as you need.

You also need to put together a packet of birdseed. Go to a pet store and buy a big bag of seed. Go to the grocery store and buy a bunch of small plastic bags. Divide the seed into a bunch of the bags to deliver with the feeder.

When you deliver the finished feeders, you can put your information and feed right inside the feeder.

Special Notes

Sell bird seed. Making the feeders isn't a one-time deal. You can become the "service agent" for the feeders as well. When you deliver the feeders, tell the customers that you'd like to be their seed supplier. Make arrangements to bring by a new bag of seed once a week. You can make your bags of seed in the same way you did before, and sell them for maybe fifty cents apiece.

You can make better money on your seed if you buy it in big containers and then divide it up into several small containers to sell.

"What does a 200 pound canary say?"

"Here, kitty, kitty!"

Grocery Delivery

Taking orders and delivering groceries to people who can't shop for themselves

Many older people can't get out to the grocery store very much. But they need to eat just like the rest of us. They're often willing to pay someone else to do their shopping for them. They write up a list of things they want, give the list and the money to their shopper, and then wait in the comfort of their home while the shopping's done.

You can do a real service by delivering groceries to people's homes, saving them both time and effort.

How to Do It

Find customers. The first step, of course, is to find people who need shopping done. I've already mentioned that older people are good candidates. So are mothers with new babies. So are working women, who often don't have time to go shopping for themselves.

When you decide to do grocery delivery, pick a day or two per week you'll do your work on. Then make up a flyer that will help you attract customers. Go door to door with your flyer. If you can do it, talk to the people personally, so they'll see that you're someone they can trust with their money. Then leave them the flyer, so they'll have your name and address when they want shopping done. Or, if no one's home, just leave the flyer at the door.

In addition to handing out the flyers, consider contacting some of your local clergymen. They'll know of some shut-ins and elderly people who might welcome your service.

43

Set a price. The customers are going to want to know how much you'll charge. You can charge by the trip if you want. Some kids do just that (like 50 cents a trip for short trips) and they do very well. But it might be better to charge a percentage, say 5 or 10 percent of the price of the items you buy. That means if you buy a $2 item with a 5 percent charge, you'll get paid 10 cents. That's not too much. But what if you buy $50 worth of groceries with a 5 percent charge? You'll get $2.50 for your effort. And if you charge 10 percent for those two purchases you'll get 20 cents on the first and $5 on the second.

Some kids charge 10 percent on smaller purchases and 5 percent on larger ones. That approach works too.

 Take the cost of the beans you pick up, figure a percentage, and you've got the amount you charge the customer.

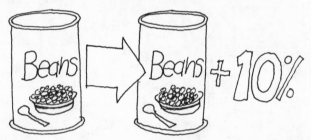

Find transportation. If you live five miles from the store and you have only your feet to take you there, you should probably find another line of work. Transportation is crucial to success in this business. It will determine how much you can make and how fast you can make it. If the store is just down the block, you'll probably be all right afoot. With large orders, the store may let you borrow one of their shopping carts to deliver the groceries, especially if you return it right away. But be sure to get permission before you take the cart away from the store premises.

If you have a bike with a basket, you can travel farther to the store—but you'll be limited in the amount you can pick up per trip. A wagon may also do the trick.

Take special care not to break anything—you'll be responsible for the cost of the item! If you live quite a ways from the store, or if you want to make big purchases for your customers, you'll probably need the help of someone with a car. Either get a parent who's willing to sacrifice a little for your money-making venture—or find someone who's willing to help for a cut of the profits. One approach that might work is to set your shopping day the same as your mom's or dad's. Then you can just do your shopping at the same time and the transportation problem will be solved.

Take orders. Once you've solved all the preliminary problems, you need to start taking orders for groceries. All the difficulty will be in getting started, right at the first. Your flyers and personal contacts should get you over that hurdle. Once you've gotten started, you'll be able to have a steady job. Prove to people that you are dependable and they'll rely on you every week. You should generally deliver the groceries on the same day as you take the orders. And if you're picking up perishables, be sure to get them to the buyer without delay.

In taking orders, be sure that you get the people to be specific. Ask them to write it all down for you, including brand names, sizes, and quantities. Also ask them what you can substitute if the store doesn't have what they've listed.

Special Notes

Expand to other items. Groceries are just one thing people need on an ongoing basis. Once you've established yourself with your customers, ask them what else you can get for them. Some suggestions:

- drugstore items: medicines, toiletries, and so forth
- postage stamps
- books (from the library or bookstore)
- stationery and envelopes, pens and pencils
- dime-store-type items: shoe laces, light bulbs, magazines, candy
- and whatever else you can think of

Look for things that block or hinder people from going to the store, and you'll have found your customers. Good indications people might need your services: they're sick; they're too busy; they just got back from vacation and haven't had a chance to go to the store.

SuperIdea!

Advertising "You have to tell to sell."

"Something horrible happens to businesses that don't advertise: nothing!"

If you don't advertise in one form or another, you won't get customers. And if you don't get customers, you won't have a business. If you don't have a business, you won't make any money. And if you don't make any money, you won't be able to get the things you want and need.

There's only one way out of this mess: advertise to get the customers to give you the business to pay you the money to buy the things you want and need. The first step is always advertising.

Throughout this book we talk about several ways to advertise what you're doing. On these pages we'll put them all together for you:

- Door-to-door sales. This is advertising in person. You use your voice and your personal appearance and your sales approach to advertise your product or service on the spot. This method is time-honored and can be effective. But it has to be done right. Tell the person at the door exactly what you're up to. Use a prepared sales pitch—but don't sound like a tape recorder when you give it. Keep it short. Speak clearly. And follow these precautions: watch for traffic, stick to neighborhoods you know, and generally avoid entering the customer's home.

- Flyers. These are cheap and easy to do. Write or type on a piece of paper what you want people to buy. Make it sound inviting, so they'll be interested. Tell them your name and phone number, so they can call you. Make it look as attractive and professional as you can. If you have artistic

46

skills, or if you know someone who does, put a picture on
the flyer. Or get one out of a book. (Simple line drawings
work best.) Once your flyer is ready, take it to a copy
machine and run off as many copies as you need. Take the
copies around the neighborhood you want to sell to and
stick them in the mailboxes or on the doorsteps. (Some kids
have success with door-to-door selling combined with flyers.
When they find a house where no one's home, they leave a
flyer.)

- Posters. These are effective when hung in the area where
  you've set up shop, as well as on bulletin boards and in
  windows of stores. They should have the same basic
  information as the flyers, and can look much the same, only
  bigger.
- Notices. Notices can be printed as small cards and put on
  bulletin boards in schools, supermarkets, Laundromats, and
  similar places. They tell the reader what you're up to and
  how to get ahold of you.
- Lawn signs. Stores put up signs to attract people to come
  inside. You can do the same by putting a sign on your lawn,
  telling people what you can do for them. A lawn sign can
  look like a real estate sign, painted on wood or metal, or it
  can be drawn on cardboard and be less permanent. Before
  you put up a lawn sign, check with city ordinances. Some
  places don't allow it. If your area does allow it, you might
  even expand your advertising to the lawns of friends—with
  their parents' approval, of course.
- T-shirts. T-shirts are like flyers or posters, only you wear
  them. Make them look neat and people will notice and
  remember them.
- Newspaper classified ads. Write a good ad and you'll be able
  to contact a lot of people for a relatively small amount of
  money. And you'll be able to go right to the people who are
  looking for what you have to offer, since those are the
  people who will be browsing in the ads. Rates vary from
  newspaper to newspaper, but almost always they're charged
  by the word. The shorter you can keep your ad, the cheaper
  it will be. Before you write an ad, check in your paper to see
  what the other ads look like. That will give you some good

ideas. If you need help writing the ad, ask your parents or a neighbor. In some areas, the newspapers also help people put their ads together.

- Other classified ads. Some areas have free papers that contain only ads, available in supermarkets. Such papers often have good circulation and cost less than city newspapers. Ads can also be placed in church bulletins, school papers, and the like.

- Business cards. You can get a thousand of these printed up for a small amount of money. If you want less than a thousand, it will cost you even less! Hand them out everywhere you can think of, and people will remember you.

- Business stationery. If you have your own stationery printed up, it will advertise your business every time you need to write a letter. You can even use it for personal letters. Make the stationery look attractive and professional, and people will be more impressed with it.

- Word of mouth. This is one of your best forms of advertising, and it comes incredibly cheap! Make your customers happy and they'll tell others about your business. People are always interested in knowing where they'll get a fair deal. If word gets out that you give people what they need, that you provide it for a good price, and that you're pleasant to work with, word-of-mouth advertising will go to work for you.

MoneyMaker!

Sealing Driveways

Sealing driveways is a valuable service. Every asphalt drive periodically needs to be sealed. It's not a difficult job, but it does take a little know-how. The best thing to do is go to the library and study up on it. Here's the main idea:

1. Clean off the driveway with a hose and broom.

2. Apply the sealer (a chemical mixture that comes in a can) with a brush. The sealer is available at lumberyards and building supply places.

3. Squeegee the surface to even it all out.

Before you try to seal driveways for pay, you should probably volunteer to do it for free on a couple of driveways, just to make sure you can do a good job. That experience will also help you know how long it takes and give you an idea of how much to charge.

Make Things with Scraps

Sew clothing scraps into hot pads and pot holders, placemats and napkins

Most people just throw old clothes away. Some hand them in to thrift stores, like Salvation Army or Goodwill. And still others see throwaways as a money-making opportunity: they collect the rags that other people have gotten rid of and turn them into things that they can sell. It doesn't take a lot of skill; it takes very little equipment; and those "scraps" (now useful items) can bring a good market price.

How to Do It

Create a pattern. Patterns for scrap-sewing come in all varieties—some are simple and some are fancy. If you want to get fancy, you'll need to have some experience with sewing. Then you can create your own pattern, or get some ideas from a library book.

But it's best to start simple. Here are a few items you can make:

Hot pads: These come in different sizes. Check the ones in your kitchen to see which you like best—or ask your mom which one works best for her. Once you've decided on the size of your pads, cut two squares of cloth the same size, and lay them face to face. Sew up three of the outside edges. Then turn the hot pad inside out (which will really put the *outside* out) and stuff a thin layer of cotton batting inside it. (You can get cotton batting at a fabric store.) Sew up the last side and you're done!

The better the work you do, the more money you'll get for it.

Pot holders: Some people just use hot pads for pot holders and vice-versa. But sometimes they come in different sizes. Find ones in your kitchen and make them in the same way as the hot pads.

Napkins: Napkins are nothing more than squares or rectangles of cloth, with the edges hemmed. Check what kind of cloth napkins you have in the house and pick a size you like. (If you don't have any at home, the ones in the store often tell what size they are, so you can look there.) Pick out some cloth that's attractive, soft, durable, and washable. Cut the cloth to the size of the napkins. Sew a thin hem around the edge, and you're done.

If you want to make napkins with frayed edges, just for an extra touch, sew a line around the edge, but in a little. Then unravel the threads up to the point where you're sewn.

Cloth napkins are always in demand for dinners and special occasions. Some people use them every day.

Placemats: Make these the same way you did the napkins, but the material you use for placemats should be fairly heavy-duty. It's nice if you can make matching sets of napkins and placemats, with four or six or eight per set.

Find the scraps.   You know how to sew different items now—but where do you get scraps? Start by going through your family's old clothes box; most families have one. (Maybe mom calls it her "mending box," but she hasn't gotten to it for years!) If you can't get to the old clothes box, the next place to check is with relatives and neighbors: "Do you have any old clothing scraps you could let me have? I'm making some items for a money-making project." Try to pick out scraps with bright colors and attractive patterns. Solid colors can also be popular.

Don't forget all the cheap material that's available at thrift stores like Salvation Army and Goodwill. Some places even sell it by the bagful, when they think the clothing is past hope.

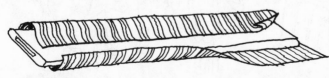

The ends of bolts of material are often the best-priced fabric around.

51

If you decide to sew with used material, make sure it doesn't have any stains. And wash it before you start to work with it.

A final place to try is stores that sell material. You can often buy ends of rolls (bolts) real cheap—and sometimes the store will have other material scraps they'd be glad to get rid of.

Make the items.   Even though you've read how to make the items from scraps, it will take some practice to become skilled at it. The first few you make might have some problems, like maybe the hem you sewed is crooked, or you wasted material by cutting things wrong. Don't get discouraged. Everyone has

problems when they just start out. Those who stick with a project like this can become quite professional—and when they do, they really start to earn their keep.

Other items you can make.   Besides the items we listed earlier, you can create and sell a number of other items. We've included a few below, just to give you an idea. You can get details at the library on how to make all kinds of household items, decorations, even toys.

Sell your creations.   There are a number of places where handicraft items are sold. If your creations are high quality, you should be able to get money for your crafts at any or all of the following:

rummage sales	church bazaars
flea markets	community bazaars
garage sales	kids' craft sales
door-to-door sales	swap shows
arcades	boutiques

Usually the rummage sale or flea market or garage sale will be one that someone else is putting on. But they'll usually give permission for another person to sell items also. They may charge you a small percentage (up to 25 percent), or they may let you sell for free.

Another place to consider is local gift shops. You may be able to get them to sell your items on consignment. That means they'll sell a batch for you, taking a percentage of the sale for themselves. They won't pay you until the items are sold, and if they don't sell, you'll have to take them back.

SuperIdea

Do Something Extra *Whenever you've agreed to do something for someone else, always do a bit extra.*

Say you've agreed to clean their basement. You're supposed to clean out all the junk, and they're supposed to pay you for it. No one has said anything about sweeping and mopping the floor. But do it anyway. That's a nice little extra touch that will mean a lot.

Say you've agreed to walk someone's dog. You're supposed to take the dog out for a half-hour stroll around the local points of interest—and they're supposed to pay you for it. But do something extra: give the dog a good brushing, to make him feel better and to make his coat look cleaner and fresher. You'll get your money if you don't do that, of course—but if you do, you can bet the owner will notice and be pleased.

Whenever you try to sell something, always give them a little extra.

Maybe you're selling apples on the corner. A customer comes up to buy a batch. As you hand him the bag, stick a couple extra on the top. He'll feel—and he'll be right!—that you're giving him extra. And he'll want to come back again.

Maybe you're selling calendars. You take orders from the people, and then you buy the calendars they wanted. But you decide to also include a little extra—you arrange with a local merchant to distribute some of the promotional calendars he's had made up. When you take the calendar the customer ordered, you also take the promotional calendar, free of charge. Everyone likes two for the price of one!

Whenever you make something to sell, always do a little extra on it.

Imagine you're making aprons from scraps. You want the aprons to look good and last long. So instead of putting only one set of stitches along the seam, you put two. That's something extra that will really make a difference in the quality of the apron.

Imagine you're making arrangements of dried flowers. You put in the flowers you've gathered, nicely arranged. Then you add your "extra" touch: you put on a ribbon. It doesn't cost much, and it sure does add to the attractiveness of your arrangement.

Whenever you do anything for anyone, always try to do a little extra. There are some good reasons for this:

It will make you feel good. We always feel better when we do something for another person—especially when we don't have to.

It will make the customer glad that he's buying the product or service from you. When you give him that and more, he'll notice—and be impressed.

It increases business. When someone gives good service or good products, people notice. They want to come back for more.

It's good advertising. People who are happy with a business tell their friends about it. And when the friends are happy, they tell *their* friends. Doing something extra for customers can be an inexpensive way of advertising.

It builds good habits for your working career. When you're older and you go to work for someone else, you'll be in the habit of doing something extra. It will be easy for you to do extra things for your new boss or your new company. The boss will notice—and he'll be happy he hired you!

Make and Sell Easter Items

Make Easter eggs and candy and sell them; sell other items at the same time

Easter rolls around every year—and every year parents need new things to give their kids. After all, it just wouldn't be fair if the Easter bunny didn't show up!

It seems like every year, shortly after Easter, many children accidentally wreck their Easter baskets. They eat up all their candy. They crack and consume their Easter eggs. The grass that goes into the baskets gets scattered arou. I the house.

By the time the next Easter shows up, the parents need a whole new batch of stuff. How nice it would be if some enterprising kid showed up at the door selling what was needed!

Most little kids are like mine: they ruin their Easter baskets (and fake grass) every year, and need new stuff for the next year.

How to Do It

Gather materials and merchandise. First you need to make a decision: are you going to sell only things put out by manufacturers, or are you going to make some of your own things too?

For example, one man who got together with some kids in a youth project for Easter. They bought some chocolate and some molds from a candy store and made their own Easter candy. And they were pleasantly surprised at the price they could ask when they sold it door to door.

Or you might want to color eggs for parents. With a little

Put on a special outfit when you go out to sell—you might feel silly, but it sure sells merchandise!

practice, a person can learn how to make all sorts of fancy eggs. And many parents would welcome the chance to buy colored eggs without having to color them all themselves.

In addition to things you make, you could peddle other Easter items, like we mentioned above. Possibilities:

manufactured candy
stuffed toys (chicks and bunnies are favorites)
Easter baskets
fake grass to go in the baskets

You may want to take orders in advance, then deliver two or three days before Easter. You wouldn't want to invest all your money in stuffed animals—but maybe you *could* buy a couple as samples to take orders from.

Set a price. Once you've decided on the line of goods you want to sell, you'll need to set a price. Go to a few stores and see what they're charging for the same type of items. You should sell yours for a little less—that will encourage people to buy from you.

Handle the eggs with care—no one wants to buy cracked eggs!

The only way you'll be able to sell things for less than the store is if you can buy them cheaper yourself. A wholesale distributor

57

is the answer. Or make things yourself—that will be cheaper still.

Find customers.   The best place to find customers for Easter items is at their homes. Go from door to door and show them what you have available, and explain that your price is the best in the area.

Take the trouble to make up a little flyer to take with you. When you come to a door where no one is home, leave the flyer there, explaining what you have to sell and how much it costs.

Keep a list of your customers. They may be prospects for buying Christmas things at the end of the year, and you'll certainly want to see them again next Easter!

MoneyMaker!

Customized Eggs.

One girl goes all out at Eastertime—she sells customized eggs to boutiques. She pokes a tiny pinhole in each end of an egg and carefully blows out the inside. (This takes a bit of practice—you may break a couple of shells while you're perfecting your approach. Don't just waste the eggs—refrigerate them and have them for breakfast the next day!) Then she takes the empty shell and hand-paints it in bright colors. The result is quite impressive.

Her next step is to take the eggs to a local boutique. They take the eggs on *consignment,* which means they don't pay her for them until they're sold. If some don't sell, they just return them to the girl.

But every year her eggs sell out. People are so impressed with them that they are happy to pay the price. And the next year they come back for more.

Those who would like to learn how to do this kind of craft can do what this girl did: go to the library and read up on it. There's a wealth of material there.

Picking Fruit, Berries, and Vegetables

Hiring on as a helper for people who have a lot of produce to harvest

When fruits or vegetables are ready to harvest, they're ready to harvest! A delay of even a day or two can mean disaster to the farmer or gardener who has a lot of crops.

So the farmer needs to hire some help. He'll usually know in advance how much he's willing to pay—sometimes it's by the hour; sometimes it's by the amount of stuff you harvest. Whichever it is, this is a seasonal job that can pay you well for a few day's work. The work can be hard (bending, stooping, stretching, carrying); you'll certainly earn your money. But a few sore muscles will be worth the extra cash.

How to Do It

Find customers.   Your customers are farmers or gardeners who have a lot of stuff to harvest. You'll need to start early, before the picking season rolls around. Otherwise the farmer may make other arrangements and you'll be left out in the sun without a job.

It's rare that a farmer sees an eager beaver—be one, and he'll be impressed.

Check around at the local orchards to find out what kind of need they'll have for help in the upcoming harvest. Talk to the farmer or foreman and tell him you'd like to work.

Or you might check around with people in your neighborhood who have large garden areas or several fruit trees or berry patches. "I'd like to help you pick your fruit, vegetables, or berries," tell them. If you've been helping them throughout the summer on their garden or orchard you'll have an even better chance of getting on.

Agree on a price.   Farmers already know what they want to pay. They hire help all the time at harvest time, and they know what the going rate is. What you need to do is ask in advance what he's going to pay, so you'll know what to expect. If you work for a neighbor, call some farmers to find out what their going rate is. Then you can charge your neighbor that amount. And maybe because he knows you he'll even pay a little more!

Do a careful job.   Nothing is worse than bruised fruit or squashed berries. The farmer will probably give you instructions about how to pick the fruit and put it in the basket or box; if he doesn't, ask for some. Whatever you do, *don't drop* the fruit, place it gently in the box.

At the same time, be careful with yourself—climbing trees and ladders, as well as carrying heavy bushel baskets, calls for caution!

Special Notes

Buy fresh fruit and sell it.   This job gives you an opportunity to make money at another job: selling some of the fruit yourself. Now that you have an "in" with the farmer, ask him if you can buy some of the fruit wholesale, at the same price he'll be charging the stores or fruit outlets or farmers' market. Once you've purchased some fruit, you can sell it door to door, or ask your dad or mom to sell it to people they work with. Fruit is always a popular item, and if your price is right you won't have any trouble selling what you have, and making a little profit besides.

Give out samples and your fruit will sell even faster.

Addressing Houses

Installing street addresses on homes

Every home should be easily identified by its address. That makes it easier for everyone: letter carriers, visitors, special delivery people and so on. But not every house has an address marking that's easy to see.

You can earn some extra cash by helping people put addresses on their houses. It's a service many people will be thankful for and it isn't that difficult to do.

How to Do It

Find customers. Customers for this business are easy to spot: just walk down the road and look at the addresses as you go by. If the address is missing, or if it's hard to see, you've got a potential customer. Go up to the door and introduce yourself. Tell them you'd love to put their address on their house, and that your charge is very reasonable. Some people won't be interested. But many will.

It may help to give the homeowner a little sales pitch. "Your number is hard to see from the street. When visitors come, they probably have a hard time finding your house."

Set a price. Before you can set a price, You'll need to know how much the numbers cost in your area. Go to your local hardware store or lumberyard and look around. You'll see there are several kinds of numbers you can choose from:
- plastic, which are attached with glue
- brass or some other kind of metal, which are attached with screws or nails
- metal stick-ons, which have an adhesive on the back—all you have to do is peel off some paper and stick them on
- wood, which are attached with screws or nails

Once you know how much the numbers cost, you can decide how much you want to charge. I'd recommend you give the homeowner one price—not a price for the numbers plus a price for your work. You can get your charge by taking the cost of the numbers and adding on a dollar or two.

Take orders. If you buy all the numbers before you have any customers, you'll have to have some start-up money. And you may end up with numbers you don't need.

It would be much better to buy a sample of each kind of number you want to sell. Then take the sample around to your prospective customers. "I can get you numbers like this, or numbers like this. Which would you prefer?" By taking orders in advance, you'll be able to purchase only numbers you're sure you'll need.

Install the numbers.   Have the homeowner tell you exactly where he'd like the numbers, and have him say whether he wants them put up vertically, horizontally, or on an angle. If there are old numbers on the house, you'll need to remove them before you can install the new ones.

You may need to take a stool, if you're not tall. Adults usually like things at *their* eye level, which means the numbers will be about five feet off the ground, or maybe a little higher.

You'll also need to take some small nails and a hammer, if you're going to use the nail-on variety of numbers. If you try to practice on the customer's house, you might miss a time or two and make a mark on the side of his house. It's best to get some advance practice with the hammer—stand a board up against your house or fence (wherever your parents give permission) and nail a few numbers up before you go out to sell your service.

Addressing Curbs and Gutters

Putting addresses on curbs in front of people's houses

Even if a house has an address on it, it can still use an address on the curb or gutter. Gutter addresses are helpful for two reasons:

1. People can easily see them from their cars. They don't have to pull into the driveway, or get out and walk to the house if the address isn't visible from the street.

2. People can see the addresses at night. If the address is put on with fluorescent paint, visitors can shine their car headlights on them and see exactly where they are. Even highly visible house addresses are hard to see at night.

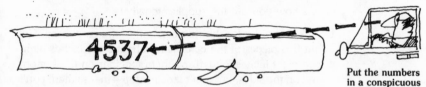

Put the numbers in a conspicuous place, so people in cars can easily see them from the road.

Most people like the idea of gutter addresses, once they've learned about it. But they aren't always equipped to put on their own. By saving them the trouble, you make yourself some extra cash! (Some cities may have ordinances controlling curb addresses. Be sure to check with your city officials before you go to work.)

How to Do It

Find customers. This kind of job works best if you can do it to a bunch of houses in a row. So to find customers you should go to an area that doesn't have any gutter addresses—or that has very few.

Once you've found such an area, go from door to door. "I'm putting on gutter addresses for people in the area. The gutter address puts the house number out on the curb so visitors can easily see it from the street. And I put it on with fluorescent paint so people can see it at night. I'd be happy to do your house while I'm in the area, and I do it for a very reasonable cost. Would that be okay?"

If they say it's okay, make sure you have the right number for their house. Then tell then you'll be back in a couple of hours to do the job—and make sure they'll be home. Tell them they don't have to pay until the job is done—in fact, you might want to have them check your work before they pay you.

It's probably best to line up all the customers you can on one street before you actually start to apply the numbers. Do all your door-to-door sales work, *then* do all the painting.

Learn how to apply the numbers. First, you'll need to have the right supplies. I'd recommend:
- a can of fluorescent spray paint
- some masking paper—typing paper or newspaper
- some heavy cardboard (cut off of a box)
- number stencils, about four inches high (buy at an office-supply store).

Here's how you put the supplies together:

1. Make a holder for the numbers out of the cardboard. Cut out two pieces of the cardboard, about three inches high and eight inches long. Tape them together on the bottom and on the sides, but don't tape the top—that's where you'll stick the numbers.

2. Cut out the stencil numbers you'll need and put them in the slot in the top of the cardboard holder.

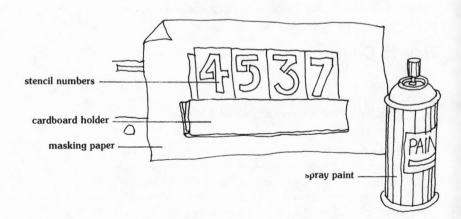

stencil numbers

cardboard holder

masking paper

spray paint

3. Mask around the numbers with the typing paper, taping it to the curb so the paint won't get on the curb. Make sure you've put it on straight. Then spray the number holes with spray paint.

4. Remove the stencil and masking and let dry.

Special Notes

Put on house numbers too. Some of your customers may have numbers on their houses, but that shouldn't stop you from talking to them about gutter numbers. And if they don't have house numbers, you should try to sell two things at once: both a gutter number *and* a house number. Every well-dressed house should have both! And if you can sell the homeowner on the idea, you'll have made two sales with one stop.

MoneyMaker!

Homemade Bread

The smell of fresh homemade bread is hard to top. And it's not that hard to make, if you find the right recipe. Experiment around until you find a kind that looks good, smells good, and tastes good—and is easy to mix and bake. (You may want to learn from someone who already knows how.) Try to learn how to make wheat bread as well as white. If you're able to give people a choice, they'll be more likely to buy. When you sell the bread, wrap it carefully so it will stay fresh.

A variation on simply selling bread is to go to offices and sell freshly baked slices of bread with butter on them, or butter and honey, or jam. If the customer likes the slice, you might be able to sell him a whole loaf to take home.

The best time to visit offices to sell your bread is during breaks or during lunch or just before workers go home for the day.

MoneyMaker!

Making and Selling Sandwiches

A kid at a Midwestern college put himself through school by selling sandwiches. He ordered a batch of 45 sandwiches from a restaurant every night, then went to a dorm and sold them all out in about an hour—for twice the amount he'd paid for them. He also sold ice cream and milk.

A kid could take that idea and really make it work. And if he also made the sandwiches, he'd make even more money. Places to sell: office buildings during lunch hour (get permission first), construction sites, college campuses, anyplace where people are hungry and food isn't handy.

Start by selling only a few, until you get an idea of how much you can sell each time. If you don't sell them all in one day, you'll probably lose some of your profits, since sandwiches are perishable. And be sure to package the sandwiches so they stay fresh—in cellophane or plastic bags.

Snow Removal

Clearing away snow from driveways and sidewalks

You wake up in the morning and suddenly it's all white outside. Your first thought might be *snowballs!* (and that could be either bad or good), but a homeowner's first thought is "Oh, no! Shoveling!"

Shoveling snow is one of those unexpected tasks that just has to be done. And it has to be done at the worst possible time: when it's cold and wet outside. To complicate matters further, homeowners in some areas can get in trouble with the law if they don't keep their walks shoveled.

If you're on the ball, though, they won't have to do the job. You can do it for them. And make some money while you're at it. And you won't mind the cold and wet so much, because you know something many adults have forgotten: snow can be fun, if you'll let it be!

The more the snow comes down, the more money you'll be able to make.

How to Do It

Dress warmly for what's sure to be a cold job. And be sure to use a good shovel—one that's lightweight as well as durable.

Find customers. The best time to start lining up customers is *before* the first snow falls. You might try going door to door and explaining your service (stick pretty close to home, since you don't want to walk far in the snow). "I'm Joe Benson, president of the Super Snow Shoveling Service, and I'd like to shovel your snow, when it comes. I'll do your walks, driveway, steps, and anything else you like. Just call this number and I'll be right over."

You don't just want to shovel snow once and then forget it, though. It's best if you can line up several customers and have an agreement to shovel their snow *every* time it comes—or everytime it gets over, say one inch. That way you can have a continuing business throughout the winter.

Another source of business is your local stores. Check with them too, to see if they need your Super Snow Shoveling Service.

Set a price. How much should you charge? It might be best to check around your area to find out what the going rate is. The charge will vary of course, according to how much area you need to shovel—and how deep the snow is. Your minimum for shoveling a small area may be 50 cents and the price can go up from there.

Special Notes

Expand to summertime jobs. Shoveling snow is seasonal work, except at the North Pole. It will keep you in money only during the winter. So you'll need something else to keep you busy during the rest of the year.

But don't despair. Now that you've worked for the people in your neighborhood and they know that you're a good worker, they'll be willing to have you do other things for them. You may volunteer to help put in their garden in the spring, take care of their yard in the summer, and rake up the leaves in the fall.

One job can always lead to another. The key is to establish a good relationship with a person, showing him that you do what needs to be done. Then he'll be willing to use you in other things.

Haul Away Junk

Loading up and hauling away all sorts of junk and
trash from people's homes

You can lighten
people's lives and
brighten their day
by hauling their
junk away!

The average homeowner collects a bunch of junk over the
years. If they tried to put it out with their garbage, the trash
collectors would rebel. Either the junk is too big to fit on the
curb, or it's against the garbage collector's policy to pick up
items that are too large or too heavy.

How do these homeowners get rid of their unwanted junk?
Either they have to find a friend with a pickup or hire some
expensive junk-hauling-away company to take it away for
them. But you can give them a third option: they can hire you
to take it away. You'll give them a service just as good as the
company's, and you won't cost as much.

How to Do It

Find customers.   The people who want stuff hauled away
are all over. All a person has to do is find them. Here are three
approaches to finding customers. One or all of them will almost
certainly work for you:

1. Make up a flyer and pass it around the neighborhood. Just
   about any neighborhood will do, except the very poor ones.
   Keep in mind that people with more money to buy things
   have more things to pitch. If you're big and strong, you may
   be able to haul anything. Otherwise, you might want to
   specify a weight limit to what you'll haul: 40 pounds, or 60
   pounds, or even 100 pounds.

2. Put up cards and posters on bulletin boards in supermarkets,
   Laundromats, and community centers.

3. Put an ad in the classifieds section of your newspaper.

Another thing you can do is be seasonal. After Christmas, check around to see if people have old appliances or old toys or old clothes or used Christmas trees they'd like you to haul away.

After big snowstorms check in neighborhoods with lots of trees to see if they have broken branches that need to be hauled away. (But don't try to remove branches that are hanging near power lines.)

In the summer, keep your eye out for people who are cleaning away shrubs and the like. Check with them to see if they need hauling help.

Be around when people are moving—that's a perfect time to get work in the junk-hauling business.

Set a price. People are going to want to know right up front how much you'll charge. Probably the best way to charge is *by the load.* Figure up how much it's costing you to use the vehicle, how much it will cost to use the dump or a dumpster, how much you want to make per hour, and how much you'll have to give others who are helping you. All that combined will tell you how much to charge per load.

You should have a minimum charge. Some people won't have a full load of junk for you to take, but you've still got the time you'll invest in driving to their place and driving to the dump.

If you can combine loads with customers who don't have a lot of stuff, you'll save yourself time and make more money.

Before you can set a final price, you'll need to determine where you'll be able to take the stuff. If your city has a public dump, that might be ideal. Otherwise, you might need to make some kind of agreement with someone who has a dumpster.

Find transportation. Before you can do anything, of course, you need to find some transportation. If you're old enough to drive, you're lucky. All you have to do is find a vehicle. If you're too young to drive, you'll need to find a partner. Ask your older brother or sister, a parent, a teenage neighbor—whoever you can find. Agree to pay them half of what you earn. They get 50 percent for helping to load and for providing the vehicle. You get 50 percent for helping to load and for providing the customer.

It's an arrangement that benefits everyone. And both partners should remember that there wouldn't be a business without the efforts of everyone involved.

If you don't find transportation right off, don't get discouraged. There are many older teenagers out there who need work. Some of them are supporting a car, and can always use more cash. Keep looking and you'll find the perfect partner.

Do the work. Be on time. Be courteous. Don't scratch up the walls when you haul stuff out. Don't try to carry too much at once. Don't agree to haul stuff that could be hazardous.

Junk hauling is natural for repeat business. After you do a job, check back with the customer. Make sure he was satisfied. Leave him a business card (you can get a batch printed up real cheap, or make your own by hand), and ask him to call when he has more junk.

Be courteous, kind, helpful, and friendly—it will get you more work and help you feel better, too.

But don't just leave it at that. Call him again in six months or so. See if he has anything new to haul.

Special Notes

Don't just throw everything away—one man's garbage is another man's treasure.

Sell the good stuff. Always have an agreement with your customers that you can sell anything you think has value. (If they balk and won't budge, you might offer them 30 percent or so of the take.) Then before you dump the stuff, go through it all and see what's there. If you think someone might buy it at a flea market or garage sale, hang onto it. That's a good way to make money twice: once for hauling away, once for selling.

If your resell business gets good, you might want to do more in salvage work. Keep your eye open for trash in the streets, in dumpsters, and other such places. Always get permission to get into things. Some people have a lucrative full-time business just collecting and reselling things that others have thrown away.

71

SuperIdea!

Use School Fads One businessman tells this experience: "I remember when I was in high school I started a yo-yo fad—without even meaning to. I bought a yo-yo one day and took it home to practice on it. I wanted to really get good on it, just because it was fun. Every night for several weeks I played around wih my yo-yo.

"Then one day I decided to take it to school. At lunch time and in the hall between classes I messed around with my yo-yo, doing all sorts of tricks with it. Other kids watched me, and made comments about how fun it would be to be good with a yo-yo.

"By the end of the week, *everyone* in that whole school had a yo-yo. Well, *almost* everyone. I was just having a good time—but in the process I started a fad that influenced the whole school.

"If I had wanted to, I could have turned that into a good money-making opportunity. When the kids would gather around to watch and would say, 'Gee, I ought to get a yo-yo,' I could have pulled out a brand-new yo-yo and said, 'Here you go. I'll sell you this one.' "

Fads are a great way to make money. I'm not suggesting you start fads to make money. That seems a little shady. But if you keep your eye out for what's happening, you might see some great opportunities. When a couple of kids bring something (or wear something) unique to school, and then a few more do the same on the next day, you know something's up. Get your business going before it's too late. Sell all you can before the fad loses its appeal.

But, if you're selling things at school, make sure you don't break any school policies. It wouldn't be worth it.

Newspaper Clipping Service

Some businesses—and some individuals—like to know what the press is saying about them. But they don't have the manpower to keep track of it. So they hire a clipping service to do it. The clipping service looks through all of the local newspapers (unless it's a *national* service) every day and cuts out the articles that mention the company. They also check local magazines. They're paid on a monthly basis.

If you like to read, and if you can read fast, you might start a clipping service. All you need to do is find one company that wants your services and you're in business. Ask around in your area, checking with the public relations departments of companies. If one business doesn't need your services, they may know of another one that does!

The customer will help you know what's expected. He'll tell you which newspapers or magazines to read. He'll tell you how often he wants you to deliver the stuff you find. And he'll suggest how he wants you to package it for him—in a notebook, or a folder, or paperclipped, or whatever.

If the customer wants you to read magazines or papers you don't get now, you can read them at the library, and photocopy the pages you need, or start a subscription.

Halloween Insurance

Insure homes against Halloween damage

People buy insurance for all sorts of things. They buy insurance to pay for repairs on their car in case it gets smashed up. They buy health insurance to pay the doctor when they get sick. They buy fire insurance to pay for damages if their house catches on fire.

And now, a whole new concept in insurance: Halloween Insurance! Actually the idea isn't all that new. Lots of kids have tried it, and it makes them good money. It helps out the homeowner too.

Some kids overdo things at Halloween—that's why there's a real need for Halloween insurance in some areas. See if any of these pranksters are familiar:

The TP Ghost

The Soap Devil

The Flat-tire Trickster

Nice Nellies and Neds (everyone isn't bad!)

Some kids get downright mean and do serious damage. If you see any, report them to the authorities.

The Garbage Goblin

The Grabby Ghoul

How to Do It

Set a price.   With health insurance, you pay the insurance company every year whether you get sick or not. But when you get sick they pay for your doctor bills.

Halloween insurance works the same way. The people pay you a certain amount. If no one messes up their house, you just keep the money. But if the house does get messed up—say someone toilet-papers it, or they soap the windows—then you have the responsibility as the "insurance company" to clean it up.

Some areas have "cabbage night," or "devil's night," just before Halloween, when kids mess things up. You might want to insure for that too.

How much is that service worth to you? I'd recommend you charge $1 per house—or $2 at the most. If you insure for cabbage night and Halloween night both, charge a little extra. If the client's house gets hit, you clean it up in the next day or two for no extra charge. If it doesn't get messed up, you keep the money without any extra work.

The best customers are those who got hit hard last year.

Find customers.   The best customers live in neighborhoods where there are older kids. Younger kids are too busy collecting candy to make trouble. But the older ones sometimes get bored with the "trick or treat" routine, and look for something else to liven up their evening.

75

There are two ways to find customers for Halloween insurance. The first is to go door to door a week or so before Halloween, explaining what kind of service you'll provide and collecting money on the spot.

The second is to pass out flyers in the area you're interested in serving. Explain in the flyer how useful a Halloween insurance can be—maybe give a couple of examples of people in the area who didn't have it last year and wished they had. Tell how much you charge. And tell them to call you if they're interested.

After the people call, go by to meet them and collect their money. Get their telephone number so you can call them after Halloween for a follow-up.

Sometimes not enough people call on a flyer like that. (In the mail-order business, advertisers figure they've done well if three out of every hundred respond. And flyers are kind of like mail order.) If you don't get enough business from your flyer, stop back by the home. "I'm offering an insurance service for Halloween—you may remember I left a flyer on your doorstep. I'd like to explain it a little more." That second stop at each house can make a lot of difference to your business.

One caution: Some crooks set up a "protection racket"—if the customer pays a certain amount each month, his business won't get robbed. But people who refuse to do business with the crooks have all kinds of trouble. They get roughed up, and their places get messed up. Kids who run a Halloween insurance business need to make sure their business is strictly honest, like real insurance is. When a kid vandalizes a house so the owner will buy insurance the next year, the kid has stopped being a businessman or woman and has become a delinquent.

Have a good follow-up. The most important thing about insurance to people is that their "agent" is available when they need him. But you can do it one better: don't wait for your customers to call you. You call them, the very next day after Halloween. "Hello, this is Sally Wilson, your Halloween insurance agent. I just wanted to make sure everything is okay after Halloween. Did you have any problems I can help you with?"

That kind of service will definitely impress the customer—and it will make them want to use you again next year, even if they didn't have a problem this year.

Holding Garage Sales

Selling a variety of items at your own garage sale

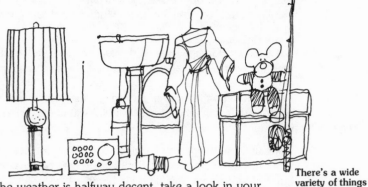

There's a wide variety of things you can sell in garage sales—most of it for a good profit.

When the weather is halfway decent, take a look in your newspaper's classified ads and you'll see a bunch of garage sales going on. The neat thing is that none of them seem to compete with each other. Just about all of them sell out of merchandise (or nearly so), and there's always room for more.

In some areas, kids have started holding their own garage sales. They've learned that with a little work and know-how, they can make some extra cash.

How to Do It

Gather the items to sell.   Start by going through all your old stuff. Pick out what you don't use or want anymore—it doesn't matter if you think it's junky, people will buy about anything.

Next, check with your folks. See if they'll donate things for your sale. If they don't want to just give it away, offer to sell it for them. They'll get 75 percent of the sale price and you'll get 25 percent.

Talk to your neighbors. Get them to donate—or to let you sell for them on the 75-25 percent arrangement.

Get your friends involved. Have them bring their stuff over. If you decide to include a couple of them in the deal, you can split your profit 50-50 with them. Or you can sell their stuff with the same 75-25 percent split. Your friends can spread the word and line up other stuff for you to sell, too.

Arrange for a place to hold the sale.   If you're doing the sale on your own, you'll probably have to hold it at your home, either in the garage (clean it up first), in the yard, or, if you live in an apartment, in the parking lot (get permission first). If a friend helps you on the sale, you might want to hold it at the friend's house. Choose the house that's closest to a good flow of traffic.

Set a time.   Garage sales work best in good weather, during daylight hours. They also work best on weekends, when people have more time to drive around and do things. They also work best when it's *not* a holiday weekend, because then people are leaving the city in droves, looking for a change of view.

Take all these things into consideration when you set the day for your sale. It can make the difference between making a hunk of money and having a big bomb.

Advertise.   This is one of the most important steps of having a successful sale. If you don't advertise, you won't get any customers. And if you don't get any customers, you might as well not have the sale.

Make your poster big and easy to see.

Try a combination of a couple of these methods of advertising:

- Put up signs in the neighborhood. This is crucial. Make them big and bright and easy to see. Put some up on busy streets nearby, with a series of signs directing people to your house. Be sure you take the signs down after the sale's over.
- Put up posters or cards on bulletin boards of Laundromats, supermarkets, and so forth.
- Pass flyers around the neighborhood. Invite people to come to the sale—and invite them to bring stuff for you to sell, if they want to. But make sure they bring it over at least a day before.
- Put a notice in your church or community paper.
- Put a notice in the classified ads of the city newspaper.

Flyers take the ad to people's homes.

Get your items out on time, and have them neatly arranged.

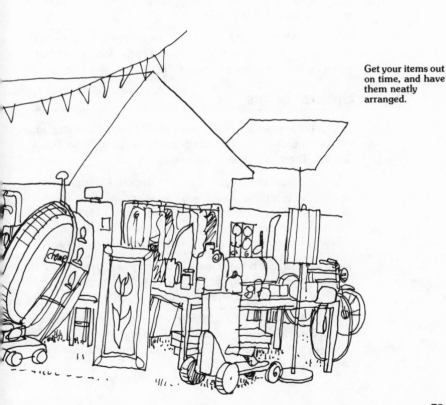

79

Set prices. Deciding on the prices for your items can be tricky. If you put them too high you'll lose money because no one will buy them. If you set them too low you'll lose money because they'll buy them too cheaply. The best thing to do is visit a few garage sales. Make notes of how much they're charging for things. If you can go back at the end of the sale, see which items are left. That will tell you if they were charging a fair price or not. It will also tell you which things aren't as likely to sell as others.

If you put a label with each item, it will help you keep better track of prices.

Set up the sale. How the sale looks makes a real difference. If things are just thrown together, people won't buy nearly as much as if they were neatly placed on tables. Make everything look neat and orderly. Clean up all the items you get; make them look as attractive as possible.

When you visit other sales for price checks, also make a few notes on how things are displayed. When you see an idea that really works, or one that you think doesn't work at all, make a note of it, so you'll remember.

When you set up your sale, have some change on hand—$20 will probably be sufficient. Then as your customers start to buy, you'll have even more to work with.

Special Notes

Sell at other places. Sometimes you'll have a lot of stuff to sell, but you don't want to set up your own garage sale. Don't despair. There are other ways to go.

You might want to visit your local flea market, for instance. (A flea market is a place where you can sell your wares after paying a small fee for the use of a table or booth.) Visit a time or two as a customer before you go as a seller. See how much people are charging and see how the whole thing works.

Another possibility is to get in on a rummage sale that a church or civic group is holding. See if they'll let you set up a table of stuff—or sell your stuff directly to them.

A third thing you can try is to go in with someone else who is having a garage sale. Price all your items and give them to the other person with the 75-25 percent arrangement. Only this time *you* get the 75 percent!

Selling Firewood

Gathering and selling firewood and artificial logs

People's heating bills are going up and up—and there's not a lot they can do about it. Unless they have a fireplace or install a wood stove. Then they can change from oil or gas or coal to wood.

People like firewood both for coziness and for heat.

But where do they get the wood? In many places it's hard to find and expensive to buy. And the idea of going out and cutting wood turns a lot of people off.

That means a good money-making opportunity for kids. They can provide the wood—or a substitute—and make the people happy, and make money at the same time.

How to Do It

Find a source of wood. You're going to have a hard time selling wood you don't have. That means the very first thing you need to do is find out where wood is available. There are many places to look. Keep your eyes open for vacant lots or farms with old trees. If you see some trees you think the owner would be glad to get rid of, ask.

Oftentimes branches or even whole trees might be blown down in big storms. If the owners don't need the wood themselves, they might be willing to let you have it in exchange for hauling it away.

Lumberyards sometimes give out scraps free or cheap, just to get rid of them—though this kind of wood is often less desirable than the harder woods you can sometimes find elsewhere.

Often adults will go out into the forest and cut trees (with a permit) for their own firewood. The more hands they can get to help them—like yours—the more wood they can collect. In exchange for your help, you'll get a share of the wood. Then you can sell your share.

While you're looking around for wood, keep in mind the need for quality. The better the wood you find, the more you can sell it for. Here's a rule of thumb: the harder the wood, the longer and cleaner it will burn. And the more valuable it will be. Examples of harder woods include the wood of fruit trees. Examples of softer woods include pines and firs. Other trees, such as elms and oaks, generally fall between those two extremes.

If you've checked around and there are no sources of wood in your area, there's still one option left: you can sell

Look for houses with fireplace or stove chimneys— and without a stack of wood by the side.

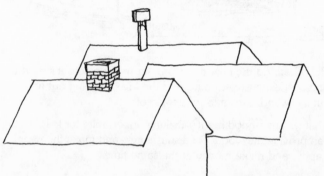

manufactured logs. These are "logs" made of pressed sawdust and other lumber scraps. Before you can sell these artificial logs, you'll need to find a source. Most grocery stores sell the logs, and so do most variety-type discount stores. If you can, make arrangements with their supplier to buy logs. Let him know you're a retailer and that you're getting the logs for resale.

Find customers.   Okay, you have the wood now—or at least you know where to get it. Your next step is to find people who are willing to buy it. Distribute a flyer in your neighborhood, or talk to the people door to door. Post a notice on local bulletin boards. Tell the people what kind of wood you have and what your price is. (You can probably charge the going rate for your area.) Let them have it at a little discount if they're willing to pick it up.

It might be a good idea to take around a piece of the wood or a sample artificial log to show the customers what you're going to be delivering. That way they won't be surprised when they see what you've brought them.

When a customer places an order, let him know when you'll bring the wood by (or when he can pick it up). Try not to buy any artificial logs until you have orders in.

Set a schedule.   Wood is something that people use all the time, like milk, and you might be able to get on a regular delivery schedule, just like the milk-deliveryman. Find out how quickly the customers will use up the wood you're supplying them—and if you have access to more, get an order to take more to them. You might be able to set yourself up with a business that will keep you in money all winter long.

You'll probably need help with transportation. Some kids have run a business like this using only a wagon (a big one), but that limits what you can do. Instead, look into the possibility of including a partner in your business. The partner (a parent, neighbor, or older friend) can help you with the pick-up and delivery of the wood, and will receive a fair percentage of what you earn.

Don't use a chain saw or an axe.   A chain saw is a pretty powerful tool. And, even though it's not a happy thought, it could take off a person's leg before he even thought to blink. Because of that, I'd recommend that you steer clear of them. The danger just isn't worth it.

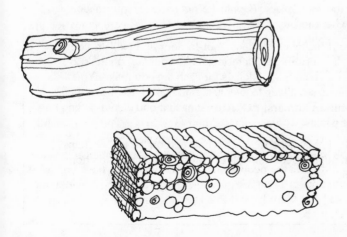

Cut the wood to standard sizes, somewhere between twelve and eighteen inches long. Some people will buy a full cord (4 feet high by 4 feet wide by 8 feet long); some will be happy with a pickup load; and some will want much less.

It's much better to find a partner and work together with a bucksaw (a two-man saw with a handle on each end). Or, if you have an awful lot of wood to cut, see if you can get an adult to help. You might want to pay him by giving him some of the wood.

An ax is another potentially dangerous tool. It takes real skill to use one effectively and safely—and a lot of the trick is being big enough and strong enough to make it work. Unless you're older (mid to late teens), you should probably *not* try to split the wood. Sell it unsplit, and let the customer split it. Or, again, try to find an adult or older kid to work with you.

MoneyMaker!

Making and Selling Pet ID Tags

Identification tags are important for pets, especially dogs and cats (goldfish don't need them as much!). But a lot of owners have never bothered to get them. By providing them, you can build yourself a good little business.

To start, you'll need to buy or rent a stamping machine. That's what's used to make the indentations in the tags. You can purchase a machine for $20 to $30. You can buy a batch of tags at the same place. (Contact a pet shop for information about where to buy these in your city.)

Take your machine and tags door-to-door and explain your service. If a customer is interested, make your tags on the spot. Charge him a couple of dollars for each tag you make. You'll only have to sell fifteen to twenty tags to make back the money you spent on tags and machine. After that you'll start getting into the profits.

Have the pet owner specify what he wants on the tag. Perhaps you can put the pet's name, the owner's last name, and phone number.

SuperIdea!

Make an Agreement Whenever you're doing something important that involves the help or payment of someone else, make a written agreement with them. The agreement doesn't mean you don't trust them—it means that you want to be sure that both you and the other person completely understand what each person is going to do. When you put things into writing, it clarifies misunderstandings and gets you both thinking the same way right at the start.

The agreement doesn't have to be complicated. It should simply say what you'll do, what the other person will do, and any other special concerns. After it's written up, both of you should sign it.

Here's a sample agreement:

"Mrs. Walker needs her windows cleaned. I, Jenny Johnson, agree to clean her windows by April 15, at a time convenient for both of us. Mrs. Walker agrees to pay me 50 cents for small windows, and $1 for large windows. She will give me a bonus of an extra $1 for her large picture window. The price is for both sides of each window. Mrs. Walker will provide all the cleaning supplies.

"Signed,

Jenny Johnson

"Jenny Johnson

Mrs. Walker

"Mrs. Walker"

Use carbon paper to make an extra copy of the agreement, or get it photocopied, so both people will have a copy.

Recycling

Collecting cardboard, newspapers, bottles, and cans for recycling

In the past few years people have become more and more conservation-conscious. They've realized that our planet doesn't have unlimited resources, and that we have to be more careful with what we have. In addition, some companies have discovered that they can reprocess old materials more cheaply than they can make new ones.

These forces have combined to produce the recycling industry of today. Recyclers take such things as used cardboard, magazines, newspaper, bottles, and aluminum cans, and make them into *new* cardboard, newspaper, insulation, bottles, and aluminum cans. But they have one big limitation: they have to rely on other people to bring the stuff in to recycle.

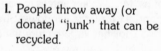

The Yellow Pages of the telephone book are the best place to find recyclers in your area.

And that's what you'll be doing in your recycling business.

Recycling comes in three steps—and you're the critical middle step. If people like you don't do the recycling, it won't happen at all.

1. People throw away (or donate) "junk" that can be recycled.

2. You pick up the stuff to be recycled.

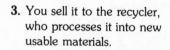

3. You sell it to the recycler, who processes it into new usable materials.

How to Do It

Find a recycler. To be able to make it in this business, it's crucial that you live near a recycler. If you have to drive 50 miles to one, recycling probably won't pay. Finding a recycler is as easy as picking up your telephone. Look in the Yellow Pages under *Recycling, Scrap Metals,* or *Waste Paper.* Most areas will have at least *some* kind of recycling going on.

Call a few of the recyclers listed in the telephone book and find out how much they pay for which kind of item. Get a complete list of what they'll accept. Also find out how the materials have to be packaged or boxed. And ask if they have a pick-up service—and if they pay you more if you deliver.

Find the items. By now you will probably know which things you want to collect, and where you'll be able to sell them. Now you need to get the items themselves. One approach is to take handbills around to all the houses in your neighborhood. Tell the people what you want them to save for you and how it should be put together (in boxes, tied with string, etc.). Don't be too demanding. Remember, your neighbors are doing you (and the earth's trees and metals) a favor. They could just as well chuck their papers in the trash as stack and tie them for you.

Tell the people that you'll collect their items periodically (like every two weeks) and that it would help if they could put them out on the curb for you.

Include your phone number on the flyer and ask people to call you if they're willing to help you out. Keep a list of those who call; keep another list of those who don't call so you can contact them again if you want.

Pick Up the Stuff. Now that you have a bunch of people saving their cans and bottles and paper (or whatever you've agreed on) for you, you need to follow your schedule to pick it up. Get some kind of wagon or bike with a carrying basket to do your rounds. Be careful with the glass and metal—either can cut you. When you've got a load, dump it in some prearranged spot—like your garage, maybe, or down in the basement. After you've gathered enough, you can deliver it to the recycler, or have the recycler pick it up at your house. (The recycler will tell you how big the batches need to be.)

A Success Story

One family really got going on recycling—and it paid off for them. In fact, it paid for their vacation last summer. That's not too bad for a little work on the side.

Here's how they worked it: Each member of the family had a specialty. James, the oldest boy, was in charge of collecting glass. Marcy, the daughter, was in charge of cardboard that could be recycled. And Hal, age six, was in charge of aluminum cans. Ronny, the baby, didn't have to do anything but watch.

Everyone helped everyone else in watching for things that could be recycled. When they'd see something, they'd bring it home and put it in the appropriate box in the garage. When they got enough of one kind of thing, mom or dad would take it in their van to the recycling center.

The individual loads didn't seem to bring much money. But then, all of a sudden, they noticed they had a hefty amount in the bank. It had added up, in little bits and pieces, until they had enough to pay for their whole vacation that summer.

SuperIdea!

What Worked Before?   One good way to find jobs that will really work is to find out what's worked before. Check around with your older brothers and sisters, older cousins, mom and dad, aunts and uncles, grandmas and grandpas, neighbors, friends' parents, and whoever else you can think of. Ask them:

- What did you do to make money when you were younger?
- How did you make it work?
- How much money were you able to make?
- Did you enjoy doing it?
- What kinds of tips would you give for me to make it work?

Find things that were successful in the past, and apply them to your own situation. You'll be surprised at what you can earn by updating some tried-and-true ideas to fit your own needs.

T-shirts

Paint, silkscreen, or iron designs onto shirts

Go into your nearest shopping center and just stand and watch the people. Take a close look at what they're wearing. A good number will have customized T-shirts on. They'll say everything from "Hug Me!" to "I'm Yours" to "Get Off My Back!" to "Red Rose Speedway." Some won't say anything; they'll just have a wild and crazy design. Or a pretty picture.

T-shirts are here to stay. They show a person's personality and it's easy and cheap to get them customized. But you can probably do the customizing cheaper than the commercial shops.

T-shirts help a person feel unique—and everybody likes that.

How to Do It

Find customers. Who likes to have their shirts customized? Just about everybody. Even rich guys get their shirts monogrammed on the pocket. But rich guys won't be the market for your customizing service. Most of your customers will be your friends and their friends and their friends—and, when the word spreads, their friends from clear across town.

An effective place to advertise is on your school bulletin board (and other schools') and in your school newspaper (and in other schools').

But here's something that will work even better: wear your best work to school. Pretty soon it will catch on. Kids will want to know where you got the great shirt. Tell them you did it yourself—and you'll do one for them for a small fee.

Another source of customers is little league teams, 4-H groups, or other clubs. They'll often buy from you in large quantities.

Set a price. First off, you should probably set a policy that you don't ever provide the shirt. Get the kids to bring their own shirts to you. That way you don't have to have an inventory of shirts on hand, which could cost quite a bit.

Another policy you should set at the same time: If you ever mess up a shirt you're working on, you'll replace it for the customer.

In setting the price for your work, check around with some of the commercial T-shirt shops. See how much they charge. Remember that they include the cost of the shirt in their charge, and adjust your fee accordingly.

You can advertise your T-shirt business on a custom-made T-shirt!

Learn how to put on the design. You'll need to do plenty of practicing before you try to charge for this service. But you can't very well practice on your customers' shirts! What if you make a mistake?

If you have some old T-shirts your parents don't care about, you can practice on them. Or you can get a batch (the size doesn't matter) from a thrift store like the Salvation Army or Goodwill.

Silkscreening takes a certain degree of proficiency. If you haven't picked it up in an art class, you can get some information from your library. But if you're not experienced in silkscreening, you'll probably be better off, at least at first, to try one of the other ways of getting words and designs onto shirts.

Painting right onto the shirt works well if you have some artistic ability. An acrylic paint, like Liquitex, is perfect for painting on fabrics. If you try this method, cut a twelve-inch square of heavy cardboard and stick it inside the shirt, then tack the shirt onto it, before you start painting. Be sure you don't poke the tack right through any of the threads, but between them.

Another way to paint shirts is to use Inkodyes. These are colors that won't fade—and they get even brighter if you let them dry in the sun. Inkodyes are perfect for painting designs. Check with your local art-supply store for either Liquitex or Inkodyes.

If you don't have any artistic ability, don't despair. You can still go into the T-shirt business with iron-ons. Local customized T-shirt shops might be willing to tell you where they get their iron-on designs and slogans.

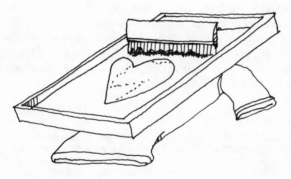

A silkscreen is like a sophisticated stencil. You put a pattern with holes under the silk, and your T-shirt under that. Then you put ink or paint on top of the silk and squeegee it down. The ink will go through the holes in your pattern and onto the T-shirt. Let it dry and you're in business!

Another thing you can do is get some patterns from local silkscreening shops. Look under silkscreening in the Yellow Pages of your telephone book and give them a call. Explain that you're looking for some patterns to mass-produce on T-shirts. Ask them if they have any on hand—or if they know where to get some. If they don't have any personally, they'll be able to help you know who to call.

Some companies are strictly in the stock pattern business. They make up patterns just to sell to other people. Find out from a local T-shirt shop or a local silkscreening company who supplies them with stock patterns. Then write to that company and get their catalog. It will have a wealth of good stuff!

You may also want to investigate other ways of decorating shirts, including embroidery, applique, and batik. The library will have information about how to do these kinds of decorations.

Special Notes

Take good care of the shirt. When you accept a shirt to do a design on, remember that you're working with someone else's property. Make sure you take good care of it—you'll lose customers fast if a shirt comes back dirty or if you've done a poor job.

Shirts should always be washed before any kind of design or slogan is put on them. Instruct your customers to wash their own shirts before they bring them in. If you have to do the washing, be sure you add on to the price. Wash in cool or warm water, not hot, to avoid shrinking.

Expand your business. When you really get good, you might want to expand your business. You can buy your own shirts in the four basic sizes (S, M, L, X-L) from a shirt wholesaler, and increase your charge accordingly. Once you reach that point, you can set up a booth at fairs, bazaars, flea markets, and malls and hopefully sell even more shirts!

A Success Story

In a western college a group of younger girls made out like bandits by selling customized T-shirts. Here's what they did: One of the girls in the group made up a fun design with the name of a dorm on it. Then they made up a few samples with the design on them—and they put the shirts on and went out a-sellin'.

They split up and went from door to door in the dorm. When someone would answer the door, they'd unzip their coats and pull them open and say, "Wouldn't you like a dorm T-shirt like this one? We can get you one for only $4."

A few of the girls in the dorm were excited about the idea, and they bought shirts. The sales were slow at first—but as the few girls who'd bought shirts began to wear them, the idea caught on. Before long, nearly every girl in the dorm had purchased a shirt. Some bought more than one shirt. Some bought for boyfriends, or little sisters back home.

And then the exciting thing happened: girls from other dorms wanted to know where they could get customized shirts too. . . .

MoneyMaker!

Window Washing

Some people hate to wash windows. It's not such a hard job—it's just that it intrudes into their normal day-to-day routine. Deliver flyers around your neighborhood and tell people you're willing to wash their windows for them. Tell them your rates (these should be a bit less than the going rate in town) and let them know you're experienced. If you're not experienced yet, get that way *fast* by helping mom out a bit!

We'd recommend that you do only windows you can reach from the ground or a small ladder. That will probably limit you to private homes—no businesses. And never lean a ladder against the window—that could mean disaster!

For suggestions on how to do a streak-free job, see the book, *Is There Life After Housework?* by Don Aslett, or another book that provides cleaning information.

MoneyMaker!

Making Candy

Homemade candy is hard to come by, but there's nothing that can match a mouth-watering piece of homemade fudge with walnuts in it! If you can make good homemade candy, or if you think you could learn, whip up a few batches and put them in attractive packages. (Be careful, though. Most candy is cooked at high temperatures.) Sell them at bazaars, flea markets (these usually don't have enough food to keep customers happy), in office buildings, and door-to-door.

Good kinds of homemade candy to sell:
- fudge
- divinity
- peanut brittle
- caramels
- peanut clusters
- almond bark

Animal Walking

Taking dogs out for a breath of fresh air and some exercise

Walking dogs can be as fun for the kid doing it as it is for the dogs.

There are millions of dogs all over this country, and every one of them needs exercise on a regular basis. Some dogs are allowed to run free, of course, so they get their own exercise. But dogs who are cooped up inside a house or small yard need something more.

Many of the owners of those dogs can't take their pets out for walks, though. They don't have the time or energy, or they just aren't interested.

For a small fee, you can take people's dogs out for walks. You get your money; the dog gets his walk; and the dog's owner gets to sit home and read the paper. It's a good deal for everyone.

95

How to Do it

Find customers.   If you live in a rural area, or even sometimes a suburban one, you might have a hard time finding customers. But in the cities and anywhere there are apartments customers are all over the place. You just have to let them know about you.

The best way to get customers in this business is to do a little advertising. Make up a flyer explaining your service, have it photocopied, and slip it under all the doors in an apartment house or two. Get permission to hang it up in pet shops, at veterinarian offices, at dog-grooming places. But don't overdo it. You might get more calls than you can handle. (Of course, then you can expand your service and hire someone to help you.)

Set a price.   The price of dog walking varies from area to area. A good length of time to walk a dog is half an hour, and you can probably charge 50 or 75 cents for that amount of time. Once you're experienced you'll be able to walk two dogs at once (unless they quickly prove they're enemies), so that adds up to four dogs an hour. Your hourly wage could come to $2 to $3.

Try to see what other dog walkers are charging in your area, before you decide for sure on your price. Call around at pet shops and pet grooming places for information on what the going price is.

Make a schedule.   It's best if a dog can be walked every day. Some owners will be willing to pay for that—and some will want it only a couple of times a week. If you're willing to work every day, you'll almost certainly be able to find the work.

The key is to make a schedule. When you hire on with the dog owner, ask how often you can come to walk the dog. If he says every night, great! But if he wants it every other night, then maybe you'll want to find another dog owner who wants his dog walked every other night too, so you can alternate.

Once you set up a schedule with the dog owner, be sure you stick to it faithfully. Be there on time every time. If you're sick or going on vacation find a replacement to go for you.

Special Notes

Take good care of their baby.   A dog is like a member of the family. He's cuddled and fed and bathed as carefully as a baby is. Some owners spend hundreds of dollars a year on their dog—bathing, grooming, feeding, clothing. (You've seen the poodles in sweaters!) You might want to meet and play with the dog a bit before you start to walk it. Each dog is an individual, and it helps if you can become friends with them before you start the job.

Sometimes people's pets are like one of their kids. Treat them with great care!

You should be as careful with someone's dog as you would be with their child. Here are some rules to keep in mind:

1. Always hang on to the leash. If the dog is frightened by a passing car or a loud noise, it might run away or get into some kind of trouble.

2. Never leave the dog, even if you tie him up.

3. Keep the dog away from other dogs. Most dogs are friendly—but it will be just your luck to run into a mean one who attacks your dog.

4. If possible, take the dog to dog places. Dogs like grass, trees, alleys, and so on. The dog will get bored if you take him down the same strip of sidewalk every night.

5. Take care in crossing streets. For some dogs, that's the time they choose to dart away and pull the leash out of your hand. It's also a place where the dog might easily get hurt.

6. Be sure to let the dog keep moving. Don't take the dog "out for a walk" and then spend the time sitting on a bench holding on to the leash. That's no better for him than sitting in front of the fire back at his apartment. You choose the route, but let the dog set the pace. He'll trot for half a block, stop to sniff the side of a building, walk across the way to use the fire hydrant, and then take off again. Let him get the kind of exercise he wants.

Learn city ordinances.   Some cities have strict rules about dogs. If you're going to stay out of trouble, you need to learn what those rules are. Many cities, for instance, say that dogs need to be kept on a leash. No problem—you were going to do that anyway.

But what about cities that say "No dogs allowed in park"? If your city has a rule like that, you'd better learn about it and then obey it.

Some cities say that it's illegal for a dog to use the sidewalk as a potty. Dogs don't know that rule, of course. So their owner (or walker) has to clean up behind it. Whether your city has that rule or not, it would certainly be a courtesy to everyone if you were to carry a small scooper and pail (with a lid!) to pick up your dog's leavings. When you get home you can dump them down the toilet.

Expand to other services.   When your dog-walking service is going well, you might want to contact the pet owners to offer them other services. Maybe you can give their dog a monthly bath, for instance. Or perhaps you can watch and care for the pet while they're away on vacation.

A Success Story

One spring Josh decided he wanted to make some extra money so he could afford to fly to another city to visit his married sister and his nieces and nephews, who were just about his age. He investigated the different kinds of jobs he could do and finally settled on dog walking. It sounded like a fun job—he wasn't too thrilled about being cooped up inside all summer anyway.

His first step was to pass flyers around the neighborhood. Josh lived in an apartment building, and he knew that many people in his building, as well as other buildings around the area, had dogs. Dogs that were cooped up all day and didn't like it any more than Josh did.

The very evening of the day Josh distributed the flyers, he got a couple of calls. Then he got some more. By the end of the week, he had a batch of dogs lined up to walk every day.

But not enough. So he decided to make a T-shirt that advertised his service. When he walked the dogs, he wore his shirt: "Josh's Super Dog Walking Service." Then in smaller letters it said, "Call 393-7426." The result: more calls.

It took about a month for the business to get going. Then, finally, he had enough dogs to keep him busy all day. He walked two at a time, for half an hour apiece. He was always on time, and he always took good care of the dogs.

By the end of the summer he had enough money to take his trip.

But that's not the end of the story. The next year he decided to do the same thing—only bigger. He passed out even more flyers. He got return business from the previous summer. And before long he had enough dogs to keep *three* kids busy. And that's exactly what happened: Josh hired two other people to help him, took a percentage of their earnings for his trouble, and made even more money.

MoneyMaker!

Dogsitting

Everyone has heard of babysitting. How about dogsitting? It works about the same: keep the dog out of trouble, feed it on time, let it go potty on time.

If you have a dogwalking business, it's an easy step from there to dogsitting. Let your customers know that you're available to take care of their dog when they go out shopping. Or when they go on a two-week vacation.

Rates are a little lower than for babysitting.

MoneyMaker!

Sell Homemade Cookies

Everyone loves a homemade cookie. And no one gets enough of them. If you're skilled with a bowl, a mixer, and an oven, fresh cookies could be a good way to pick up some extra cash.

Here's a good way to run this business. Make a few dozen cookies—no more than you can sell in one day. Wrap them in plastic so they'll stay nice and fresh. Then go door-to-door selling. Or office-to-office. Put on your best smile. Explain that your cookies are *fresh*, and oh-so-delicious! Wear a Bob's Bakery T-Shirt, if you can. If your price is right, you'll almost certainly be able to sell all you made.

How do you set your price? Add up the cost of all the ingredients. Add in the time it took you to cook them. Add in the time it takes you to sell them. But make sure you're not charging more than the bakery on the corner. Sell the cookies in batches of a dozen. You could have some bags of one kind, some of another kind, and some mixed. The more attractive your package, the more cookies you'll sell. Make sure you choose packages that will keep the cookies fresh.

In general, you should stick with the old favorites: sugar cookies, peanut butter cookies, chocolate chip cookies. It might also pay to bake some extra-fancy cookies, where you add a double portion of chocolate chips or nuts. You'll want to charge more for these—but many people will be willing to pay for the extra treat.

SuperIdea!

Making Profits   I think most people would agree with me that making profits is a super idea! If you can't make profits in your business, you'll probably want to find something else to do.

How do you figure profits? Here's a simple way: first, figure the cost of your time. That's what you think you should make per hour, and it may vary from job to job. Once you have that figure, add on the cost of all your expenses. The figure you end up with is the basic cost to keep your business running. Now add on an *extra* percentage. That's your profit. That's what makes you want to have the business in the first place.

Let me give you an example. Say you want to put house numbers on people's doors. First you take the price of the numbers: $1.25. Then you take the price of your labor: 75 cents (you can do five houses in an hour). That gives you a total expense of $2 per house, just to keep the business running. Then, to make it *profitable* as well, you add on another 10 percent (this also may vary from job to job), or 20 cents, giving you a total charge of $2.20.

Look at anyone in business, anywhere. Whether he's selling bicycles or bike repairs or school books or groceries or popcorn at the movies, you can bet he's added on that percentage for profit. If he didn't, his business would die.

Profits keep prices down for everyone. And they help businessmen stay in business.

If you want to make your business profitable, don't forget to figure a profit into what you charge!

Laundromat Services

Washing, drying, folding—or just watching—clothes in the Laundromat

Lots of people have to go to the Laundromat because they don't have their own washer and dryer—and it cuts a big chunk out of their day. They have to go there and sit and wait for their clothes to wash before they can dry them. Then they have to sit and wait for the clothes to dry before they can fold them. And they have to fold them before they can take them home. (Unless they like wrinkled clothes).

And all the while they were wishing they were somewhere else.

You can do their laundry chores for them while they go shopping, or run errands, or just go home and wait. (It's better to wait at home for your clothes to get done than it is to wait at the Laundromat.) They'll love your service so much that they'll pay you for it. You can't ask more of a job than that!

Folding clothes isn't exactly glamorous—but it can put some dollars in the pocket.

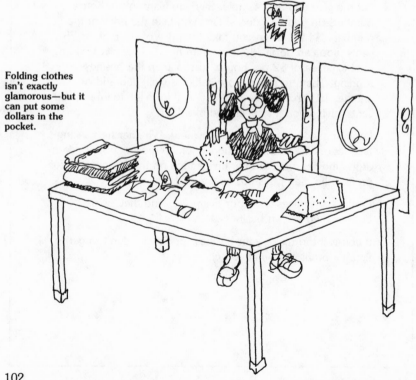

How to Do It

See the manager.   It doesn't work to just go into someone else's business establishment and set up your own business. That's a bad business practice. It'll probably get you thrown out besides. So go to the manager of the Laundromat. Make him a deal: "I'll make your customers happier by providing them a service. I won't bother anyone. It will probably bring more customers to your Laundromat. And I won't charge you anything besides."

If you can arrange to help the manager directly, you'll have a more steady source of income.

That's a deal few people can pass up. If the manager wants to pass it up, fine. There are other Laundromats in the world. He's just lost a good opportunity. But if he doesn't pass it up, you're in business. Move along to the next step.

Set a price.   Decide how much you want to charge. Don't set your rates too high, or no one will want to use you. When you set your rates, remember that you'll be able to serve several customers at the same time. While one customer's clothes are washing you can be transferring another customer's clothes to the dryer. Then while those clothes are drying you can fold a third customer's clothes. Be sure to keep things moving. And if the Laundromat is really busy, you might want to get a helper to help you meet and serve the customers.

How much do you charge, then? I'd recommend that you charge *by the load.* Get them washing for 10 cents a load. Transfer them to the dryer and get them going there for 10 cents a load. Take them out of the dryer and fold them for 25 cents a load. Be sure the customer gives you enough money for the machines.

103

Find customers. After you get the manager's okay, put up a couple of signs. Put one in the window and a couple more on tables in the Laundromat. Make each sign as attractive and colorful as you can, to catch the customer's eye.

Then you'll probably want to set up a headquarters somewhere in the Laundromat, where the customer can find you. It wouldn't hurt if you wore a little tag on your shirt or blouse, identifying you: "Official Worker in BETTY'S LAUNDRY SERVICE."

You'll be able to get most customers if you set a standard time to be there. Put the time on your signs—and then be prompt and regular. If you say you're going to be there Saturday morning from 8 a.m. till noon, be sure you do it. If for some reason you can't make it one Saturday, send a replacement, with your tag on his or her front.

One effective way to advertise is on your T-shirt.

Once you have your customers, you'll want to keep them happy. Find out exactly what they want you to do with their clothes. Learn how to use bleach and softeners, in case a customer wants you to put them in with the load. Ask how long each load should be dried—too short will leave the clothes damp; too long may damage certain fabrics. And figure out a method of keeping the customers' clothes separated from each other. You may want to use a log that shows whose clothes are in which machine.

Find out exactly what the customer wants and how she wants her clothes done.

Before   After

104

Cleaning Swimming Pools

Killing algae and clearing debris out of home and motel pools

Not everyone has a swimming pool, but people who do have to keep them quite clean. If they don't they lose the enjoyment of having a pool. And they can get diseases from dirty water, too.

Sometimes people who own pools don't have time to clean them out. It's not a hard job, but it does take a while to do. And it has to be done regularly—water doesn't take long to get dirty.

That opens up a money-making project for dependable kids. They can clean the pool, and get paid for it—and maybe even get swimming privileges as a bonus!

How to Do It

Find customers.   The first trick in finding a customer is to find out who has pools! That's not as hard as it may sound. If your parents own a pool, for instance, it's a pretty safe bet that others in the neighborhood will have pools too. Pools run in packs. If you can find one, you'll probably be able to find others nearby.

Most people who can afford a swimming pool can also afford to hire someone to clean it.

105

The best place to look is in richer neighborhoods. Go from door to door and ask if they have a pool—or if they know anyone who does. Another place to seek customers is among motel owners. With just a little checking, you'll soon have a good list of pool owners.

The next step is to get hired on as a cleaner. Tell them the services you'll provide. Point out how much time you'll be able to save them. If you can bring your own equipment, use that as a selling point—but that probably won't be necessary, since most people have their own.

The best way to set your price is to ask around, to see what the competition is charging.

Set a price.   Call up commercial pool-cleaning companies in your area and get a quote on what *they* charge. Ask for their price on a typical-sized pool, say one that's 15 feet wide by 25 feet long. You'll probably be able to clean the pool for quite a bit cheaper. Tell your prospective customer how much you'll charge—and give him a comparison of your price with the commercial company's.

Set a schedule.   Pools need to be cleaned periodically to be kept in shape. Talk to the pool owner and ask when he wants you to come by. "I can come by on Wednesday or Thursday evening or Saturday morning—which would be best for you?" Then find out how often he wants you to come. If the pool is inside a locked fence, make sure someone will be there to let you in.

Special Notes

Learn how to use the equipment.   If you've never cleaned pools before, you'll need to learn the correct procedure to get it done right. How do you learn? Probably best is to be honest about your lack of experience: "I've never cleaned a pool, but I'm dependable and I learn fast." Then ask the pool owner if he'll show you how to do it when you come over the first time—for free. (It's not fair to charge someone to teach you how to do your job.) All you need is one pool owner to teach you how to clean the pool, and most likely you'll be set up with all the other pools you've lined up, forever. Be sure to take good care of the equipment, whether it's the pool owner's or yours. If it's well cared for, the equipment should last for years—it's your responsibility to see that it does.

Don't try to use equipment you're not familiar with. If the equipment is new to you, ask for a quick demonstration.

Also be careful with any chemicals you might be using in cleaning the pool. They won't hurt anything if they're used properly—but be sure you keep them off your skin and away from your eyes. If a small child is playing nearby, keep an eye on your chemicals and equipment, to make sure the child doesn't get into them.

Start early in the season.   The first warm day of summer the guy with the swimming pool is going to want to be out there taking a swim. And it won't be too long after that before the pool needs its first cleaning. Many pool owners get quite a few offers to clean their pools for the summer. Who gets the job? The first person who makes the offer. For that reason you should talk to the owners early in the season, maybe even as early as mid-spring. Get some commitments then, even though you won't start your job until a couple of months later. (Some places use pools year-round. If you live in Phoenix or Miami, you might be able to get yourself a year-round job.)

Know how to swim.   You don't have to know how to swim to be able to clean a pool. But it's probably a good idea. Sometimes the area around the pool gets wet. And sometimes the person cleaning the pool slips and falls in. If he doesn't know how to swim, he might drown. It would be much better if he simply knew how to swim to begin with.

You'll be a lot safer around the pool if you first learn how to swim.

MoneyMaker!

Start a Go-fer Business

Go-fer businesses are built on the ground level. But not the underground! It's not too hard to be a go-fer. All you have to do is go-fer this and go-fer that. For example, maybe your customer wants someone to pick up his mail for him. Well, you just go-fer it and bring it back to him.

Or maybe you have a customer who needs some things delivered, but he doesn't have time to do it himself. So you go-fer him and do the deliveries.

You get paid for your go-fering, or course.

There are all sorts of businesses (and people) that would be interested in this kind of errand service. Small stores of all kinds often need someone to run errands. So do busy businessmen and women. So do older people, and invalids, and busy homemakers.

All it takes to get started is a little asking around: "Could you use someone to run errands for you? Do you need a go-fer?" Ask your parents, and their friends, and *their* friends. Stop in at shops and stores and ask. Check with your clergyman to see if he knows of anyone who could use the service. Check around the neighborhood. Before you know it, you'll be go-fering to your heart's delight!

Selling Kindling

Gathering and selling kindling to people with fireplaces and wood stoves

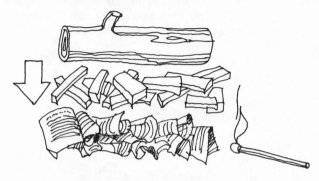

Kindling is essential for starting fires. You can't light a log with a match—but if you light the paper and the kindling, they'll light the log for you.

People with fireplaces and wood stoves use up a lot of wood. Every year they go into the forest and cut a couple of cords to use, or maybe they buy it by the pickup load from someone else.

But there's something nearly everyone always forgets. To get the wood started on fire they need some kindling. Kindling isn't advertised and sold as much as firewood is. But it's just as important to a good fire. You can be the one in your area to sell the kindling.

How to Do It

Find a source of kindling.   Kindling comes in several sizes and forms, from twigs to branches to wood scraps. Logs for burning are usually three inches in diameter or more. Kindling will usually be two inches in diameter or less. There are several places to look:

1. If you live near a sawmill, arrange with the management to get their scraps.

2. If you live near a forest or wooded area, you can probably get permission to pick up small branches and twigs that will work well as kindling.

3. Most lumberyards have a good amount of small pieces of wood that they throw out each week. You may be able to arrange to get some of it for your business.

4. Construction companies also throw away quite a bit of wood scraps, which would be perfect for kindling.

Gather the kindling into units.   No one wants to buy loose pieces of kindling. You'll need to put it into some kind of a package. There are two ways to go here. If the kindling is in long strips (1 to 2 ½ feet long), you can tie it into bundles with twine. If it's in small pieces, you'll probably need to put it in a box to sell it.

If you put the kindling into clean boxes (packaging!), it will increase the value of what you're selling.

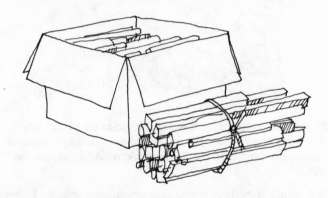

Set a price.   The price for kindling will vary from area to area, just as wood does. But, in general, you can probably charge between 50 cents and $2.00 for a bundle of wood. Bundles should be wrapped so they're about eight inches across on the end. The price of a box will depend completely on how big the box is.

The best way to tell if you·have a fair price is whether or not people are buying your wood. If no one's interested, ask a few customers what they think the kindling is worth. That will give you a better idea of what you should charge.

Find customers.   Not everyone is going to be interested in kindling—just those who have a fireplace or wood stove. If you try to sell your kindling door to door, go only to places that have a fireplace or wood-stove chimney. (Wood-stove chimneys are usually large metal pipes with a "cap" on them.) That will save you the time and trouble of stopping at doors where the people don't have any use for your product.

You can also try advertising. Put a notice on a supermarket or Laundromat bulletin board. Put a notice in wood stove stores. Try to advertise where people sell wood.

Or you may want to pass some flyers around, dropping them off on people's doorsteps. The flyer can tell the people how much kindling they'll get for their money, whether you'll deliver or they have to pick it up (delivering is best), and how to place an order.

Once you've lined up some customers, see if you can get some repeat business with them. Offer to bring by a new batch of kindling every Saturday, for the same price. Once you get a satisfied clientele, you might not need to look for new customers anymore.

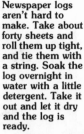

Newspaper logs aren't hard to make. Take about forty sheets and roll them up tight, and tie them with a string. Soak the log overnight in water with a little detergent. Take it out and let it dry and the log is ready.

Special Notes

Also sell artificial logs and newspaper logs.   Since you're in the firewood business anyway, you might as well get going big. That means when you sell your kindling you can sell artificial logs or homemade newspaper logs at the same time. That way you'll be killing two birds with one stone—and you'll be making twice the money (maybe more) with one stop! For more details, see the section entitled *Selling Firewood*.

A Success Story

Todd went to a lumberyard to get scraps for kindling. The people there were happy to give him permission to pick up whatever he wanted. Every week he'd go by and get wood to sell to his customers—and every week the people at the lumberyard got to know him better and better.

One day after he'd been gathering kindling for a couple of months, the manager of the business called him in to his office. "We've been watching your work, Todd, and we've been impressed. You come by every week and you always seem to really care about getting your customers the wood they need.

"We need someone to help us clean up the lumberyard a couple of times a week. Would you be interested in helping us out?"

All Todd was doing was serving his kindling business. But in doing a good job there, he was able to get a regular part-time job.

MoneyMaker!

Be a Photographer

People love pictures of themselves and their family—but they often fail to take them. Sometimes it's too much hassle for them, and sometimes they just forget. Maybe they don't feel comfortable using a camera, or maybe they've never tried using one at all. If you are pretty good with a camera, you could build a good business just taking the pictures they wish they had. Distribute flyers around the neighborhood, or advertise in the classified ads of your newspaper that you're available to take pictures at special occasions.

You can start out small, taking pictures of birthday parties. Use an instant camera, so you can give the people the pictures right on the spot.

If you don't have an instant camera, you'll need to borrow one, if possible. Practice with it before you try to sell your services, so you can be sure you're giving your customers a good picture.

Take some of your practice pictures to someone who knows about photography—a teacher, a photo store sales clerk, your parents, a professional photographer. Have them tell you the good and bad points about the pictures you've taken. Ask them to suggest ways you can improve your photographs.

Professional photographers are continually striving to improve their picture taking abilities. If someone points out that you've taken a poor photograph, don't feel bad and quit—take it as a challenge to try to do better next time.

MoneyMaker!

Be a Box Person

When people move, there's one thing they always need more of: boxes. How about if you could sell them the boxes they need? It would be a good way for you to pick up a few dollars; and it would really help them out at the same time.

Here are good places to get boxes:
- grocery stores
- fruit stands
- appliance stores
- bookstores
- stationery stores
- and other places like those.

The best place, of course, is a grocery store. They have lots of boxes they just throw out or crush. You might as well have them. You'll have to find out when the store employees stock the shelves, so you can get the boxes before they get rid of them.

Another good place to get boxes is from people who have just moved in. They had to use the boxes to move, but they may not want them anymore. You can provide a good service by taking them off their hands. And there's a real advantage to getting specially-made moving boxes: they usually fold up flat. That way you can get a bunch to store until you have a customer to sell them to.

For the folding boxes, you can charge nearly as much as the box companies in your area. For store boxes, charge less.

You can find customers for your business by watching the "For Sale" signs in the neighborhood—when the sign goes down, or when a "Sold" sign is put up, you know it's time to talk to the people about boxes. If you live in an area of apartments, get acquainted with some of the managers, so they'll tell you when people are about to move.

Spring Clean-up

Helping people clean their houses, basements, attics, and garages

No matter how hard people try, their houses still get dirty! They can clean every day, but by the time the year is over, there's still more cleaning to do than they have time for.

Then spring rolls around. It's warmer outside, so people can open the windows of their houses, fling the doors open, and really dig in and push the dust *out*. But spring cleaning is a big job, and many people put it off, just because it takes much time and energy. Those people would welcome a little help, and they'd be willing to pay for it.

But your help doesn't just have to come in the spring. The need for cleaning is year-round. And you can get paid for making it happen.

The homeowner may ask you to do a lot when you clean up—but it will be worth it.

How to Do it

Find customers.   There are plenty of homeowners and apartment dwellers who would love to get some assistance in their cleaning. They just don't know where to go for help.

A little advertising will go a long way. Make up some flyers and pass them out around the neighborhood. Put flyers on bulletin boards in Laundromats and in supermarkets. You'll almost certainly get a bunch of calls asking you to come help.

Once you've worked for someone it will be easier for you to get a job with them next time. To keep the business going year-round, you'll need to do some follow-up. Call the people you've worked with and ask if you can come help again. Pass out flyers again, until gradually you've built up enough customers that you have steady work.

Set a price.   The best way to charge for your services is by the house. Check around in your area to find out how much people get paid for cleaning services. You can charge a little less than adults are getting paid. But don't expect to get more than the current minimum wage.

Learn to clean.   Much of your work will be under the direct supervision of the homeowner. In that case, he or she will tell you what to do and how to do it. Your task will be to follow directions carefully.

But sometimes you'll be put in a room and told to go at it. "Clean this room," you'll be told, and that's about it.

Before you go, then, it's a good idea to know how to clean a room. Learn how to effectively pick up junk, how to clean floors, how to clean windows, how to clean walls. Learn how to handle your equipment and supplies.

One book that answers a lot of questions on cleaning is *Is There Life After Housework?* by Don Aslett. It's easy to find others in the library or at the bookstore. Be sure you do your homework before you try to go out and clean someone else's house.

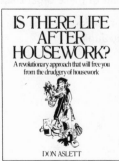

IS THERE LIFE AFTER HOUSEWORK?

A revolutionary approach that will free you from the drudgery of housework

DON ASLETT

Don Aslett's tips on cleaning can make your job easier.

115

Some of the jobs you may be asked to do:

- wash walls and windows
- sweep, mop, wax, or scrub hardwood, tile, or linoleum floors
- clean carpets, beat rugs
- clean the bathroom—toilets, tub, sink, walls
- pick up, sort through, or haul junk outside
- clean out closets and drawers
- polish silverware
- wash dishes
- dust furniture
- rearrange furniture

Special Notes

Take the junk and sell it. If the homeowner or apartment dweller is throwing out some junk, some you think you could make some money off of, get his permission to haul it away, with the understanding that you may be able to sell some of it. If he seems hesitant, offer him 25 percent of your profit.

You may need to get some adult help in a car or pickup to haul all the junk back to your house. Then you'll need to sort through what you have and decide what to do with it.

Some possibilities:

- get a neighbor to sell it for you at a garage or yard sale
- hold your own garage or yard sale
- sell it to an antique or used furniture dealer
- sell it at a flea market

If you can't get rid of it, don't just trash it. You thought there might be some value in it to start with—if nothing else, donate the junk to your local Goodwill or Salvation Army (though neither of these organizations wants garbage).

For more ideas on handling junk, see the section entitled *Haul Away Junk.*

MoneyMaker!

Cleaning Cupboards, Closets, and Drawers

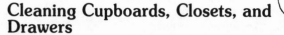

Cupboards, closets, and drawers need to be cleaned out periodically, but many homemakers are so busy that they just can't get to it.

That makes it a prime job for a kid. Offer to clean out their cupboards, closets, and drawers for them. Here's how:
- remove all the items from the cupboard or drawer
- remove the paper lining on the bottom
- wipe it out thoroughly
- put in new paper
- sort and arrange the items; have the customer help you, if possible
- put all the stuff back

Do a good job and you may be able to get other jobs with the same customer.

Party for Little Kids

Throwing all sorts of parties for all sorts of kids

Every year, most families throw at least one party for their kids. That's a lot of parties going on. And sometimes the parents could use some help in putting the party together. But they don't know where to turn.

Some kids have made extra cash by providing a party service. They advertise that they'll throw the party for the parents, and all the parents have to do is sit back and help supervise. It's a welcome relief for the folks. And it's a fun way for the kids to make money.

How to Do It

Advertise your services. You won't get much money as a party-thrower unless people know you're available. But it's not that hard to let them know. A little advertising here and there will do the trick.

Start by mentioning your services to your neighbors. If they have little kids, tell them that you'd be happy to come over and help them if they have a party coming up. Tell them the kinds of services you'll provide, and give them an idea of how much you'll charge. (You might even want to do a party or two for free, just until you get the hang of it.)

Next, call up the parents of your friends, if your friends have little brothers or sisters.

Talk to your parents' friends. Let them know what you're doing.

After you've notified everyone you know, it will be time to start doing other kinds of advertising. Put a notice on the bulletin board at nearby Laundromats, and at the supermarket. Put a notice in the local paper. And, if you still don't have enough business, put an ad in your newspaper.

Set up the party. Once you have a party to throw, figure out exactly what you'll do. You have basically three things to plan for: the food, the entertainment, and the decorations. Many books are available about all three; you can get a lot of ideas in one stop at the library. Let me get your mind going with a few suggestions:

For food, you can have one or two of the following:
- sandwiches
- cookies
- ice cream cones
- cake (this is an extra service you can provide if the parents want you to)
- fruit
- crackers
- relishes, like olives and pickles
- chips and dip
- milk
- punch

Be sure to check with the parents in planning the food. You shouldn't try to provide a whole meal—generally a snack is enough. Decide exactly what you'll bring and what the parents will bring. Don't forget paper plates and cups, plastic forks and spoons, napkins and plastic (or paper) tablecloth.

MoneyMaker!

Party Entertainer

We've talked about a party-thrower—someone who puts on parties for other people's kids. A party entertainer is different. He doesn't have to put on the whole party. All he has to do is come to the party and do his specialty.

People have made good money doing the following as party entertainers:
- being Santa Claus at Christmas parties
- being Dracula or Frankenstein at Halloween parties
- being a leprechaun at St. Patrick's Day parties
- being a magician
- putting on puppet shows
- doing skits
- leading sing-alongs
- being a game leader
- being a stand-up comic

For entertainment, consider one of these:
- puppet show
- magic show
- ring around the rosie
- pin the tail on the donkey
- blind man's bluff
- sing-along
- musical chairs

And don't forget time for opening gifts!

For decorations, try these:
- balloons
- streamers
- posters
- hats for each child
- noisemakers or party blowers for each child

Set a price.   The parents will want to know in advance how much you're going to charge, and that's going to take some careful planning. You need to charge for:
- the cost of the food, plus a little profit
- the cost of the decorations, plus a little profit
- the cost of any special items, like small gifts you may get for each child
- the cost of your time—don't forget to include any time you spend shopping for the party, as well as your time at the party itself.

Of course, you often will provide only a portion of the services we've talked about—you may only do the entertainment, or you serve the food, but the parents purchase it—and you should adjust your rates accordingly.

Special Notes

Expand to other party services.   There are several other ways you can make money from parties. Let me list a few:
- Throw a variety of kids' parties. Advertise your services for birthday parties, then expand to other kinds: Halloween, Christmas, Valentine's Day. Then get creative: New Year's Day, President's Day, St. Patrick's Day, School's Out Party, Fourth of July, Back-to-School Party, Un-Birthday Party, local holidays.
- Help prepare for adult parties. You can help by picking up

items at the store and decorating the house where the party will be.

- Help serve at adult parties.
- Help clean up after adult parties.

SuperIdea!

Make a Budget   Russ wanted to buy a bicycle. He was making a little money every week, and he figured if he saved it up it wouldn't be too long before he had his brand-new bike.

A couple of months later he added up his money to see how he was doing. It was hard for him to believe, but he didn't have much more than he started with!

What could be wrong? Russ's problem was that he hadn't been making a budget. When he got money in, he had the feeling that he was saving a good amount, but he had no idea where his money really went. He had no record.

A budget can do two things for you. It can help you know where your money's going. And it will help you plan for where it *should* go.

The first thing to do in making a budget is to add up how much money you make each month. We'll use Russ as an example. He was making $45 a month through a variety of jobs.

Next, keep a record of where you're actually spending your money. When Russ kept track, he learned he was spending the following every month:

- movies—$5
- goodies at movies—$2.50
- soft drinks, candy bars, etc.—$7.50
- video games—$10
- books—$5
- clothes—$12
- miscellaneous—$3

Russ *thought* he was putting money into savings—but he wasn't really. He "robbed" his piggy bank throughout the month until there was nothing left.

Once you know where your money is going, you can decide what to do about it. If you're happy about how things are going, maybe you can leave well enough alone. But if you wish your money went farther, it's time to do the next part of making a budget: plan your expenditures in advance. When you take this step, you set aside a certain amount of your money to buy certain things—and when that portion of money is gone, you don't do those things anymore.

Let me give you an example. Russ wanted a bike, so he decided he'd better budget for one. He had two choices—either he could try to earn more money, or he could spend less. He wasn't sure he wanted to earn more—so he'd have to sacrifice his spending and save instead. Here's what he worked up for his budget:

- savings for bike (don't touch!)—$15
- movies—$2.50
- goodies at movies—$1
- soft drinks, candy bars, etc.—$5
- video games—$5
- books—$3
- clothes—$10
- miscellaneous—$3.50

It doesn't really matter what we spend our money on—as long as it's not immoral or illegal! What does matter is that we're getting the most for our money, that we're getting the things we want and need with the money we have. Having a budget is the best way to make sure we keep tabs on what's coming in and what's going out. It's the best way to stretch our spending dollars the farthest possible distance. Budgeting is also an excellent way to maintain our personal savings program.

Selling Golf Balls

Collecting lost golf balls and selling them to golfers at the tees

Some golfers never lose a ball. And some run out before they get to the end of their game. Those that go through them so fast will give a kid a good business in two ways:

First, they provide lost balls that the kid can find and resell.

Second, they become customers for those recycled balls!

Golfers lose balls all the time. It helps to have someone recycle the balls for them.

How to Do It

Find the balls. Every day golfers lose their golf balls. If they lose them on the green (the grassy part of the course), some other golfer will find them and pick them up for himself. But if they lose them somewhere else, you'll have a chance to get them for your business. You'll probably need to see the course manager before you try it, though.

The first place to look is in the rough, which is just about everywhere on the course where the lawn isn't cut neat and trim. Look under bushes, behind trees, and in the tall grass.

The next place to check is over the fence. If a golfer hits his ball out of the course, he won't go to the trouble to go and get it. He'll just pull out another ball and continue his game. That leaves the ball just lying there waiting for someone like you to pick it up.

The last place to check, with the permission of the course managers, is in the ponds. You may need to get a swimming

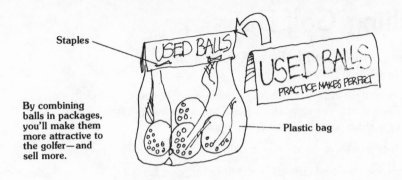

Staples

By combining balls in packages, you'll make them more attractive to the golfer—and sell more.

USED BALLS

USED BALLS
PRACTICE MAKES PERFECT

Plastic bag

suit and snorkle to do this. You'll find quite a few balls in the ponds, but don't try it unless the course managers say you can—and you know how to swim.

Set a price. Used balls won't sell for as much as new ones, of course—but all you had to do to get them was a little work. Balls that are all nicked up will sell for about a quarter apiece. Balls that are in good condition will usually sell for 50 cents or 75 cents each. And balls that are good as new will probably sell for as much as $1 each. A lot depends on what brand of ball you've found—some start out cheap, even when they're new. With a little experience you'll get to know which balls are expensive and which are cheap. That will help you know how much to charge. Clean dirty balls up with mild dishwashing detergent and warm water, and you'll be able to get more for them.

Another thing you can do in working with golfers is wax their bags and club covers with saddle soap.

Sell the balls to golfers. It's not a good idea to bother golfers when they're in the middle of playing a hole. But if you set up shop at one of the tees, you'll get all the golfers who are playing the course, and you'll get them between holes. They'll be more interested in talking to you then. (Don't forget to get permission from the course manager.)

The best place to sell your balls would be toward the end of the round, say at hole 14 or 15 on an 18-hole course. The golfers will be more likely to need new balls at that point.

Another place to sell balls is directly to the pro shop. They won't give you as much per ball as the golfers themselves will, but with the pro shop you've got a steady customer, and you don't have to spend the time selling the balls yourself.

124

Christmas Tree Stands

Making and selling stands to hold up people's Christmas trees

Millions and millions of Christmas trees are sold every year. Many people don't have stands to hold their trees up when they get home. So either the tree seller has to make stands, or the customer has to make or buy his own.

Since so many trees are being sold, kids could make some extra money at Christmastime by making stands to go with the trees. They could work with the tree distributor or directly with the customer. Either way, they'd be providing a much-needed service.

A sturdy stand can make the difference between a straight tree and a leaning tower of Pisa!

125

How to Do it

Find a tree distributor. The best way to sell tree stands is to work directly with someone who's selling trees. There are two ways to work with him.

1. Ask him if you can provide the stands for the trees he sells. If the customer wants a stand, the seller will give him one, for an added charge (maybe a dollar or two). Then you'll split the money fifty-fifty.

2. Ask him if he'll let you set up your shop right next to his. When his customers buy a tree, you'll stop them and ask them if they'd also like a stand. You can put together and sell a "stand kit" (pre-cut wood, nails, instructions) for a dollar or two, plus an extra charge if you put it on. Then you give the seller a cut of the money for every stand you sell, in exchange for the privilege of working with his customers.

Another approach is to sell your stand kits door to door. If you do this, go around early, before the people have purchased their trees. By the time they get the tree home, they've usually worked out what they're going to do for a stand.

Make the stand kits. Whether you attach the stand or the customer does, it will be easier if you first create a kit. The kit should include the wood, cut into the right shapes and sizes, the necessary nails, and if you give it to the customer, simple instructions about how to put the stand on.

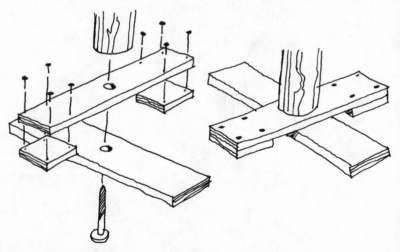

Selling Christmas Wrap

Buy Christmas wrap in large rolls, cut it into smaller rolls, and sell it for double your cost

One of the best ways to make money is to find something a lot of people need, and then sell it to them. And if it's something they really need, they'll pay you well for getting it for them.

Everybody loves Christmas. They've saved up for it for months. But what good is a gift that isn't wrapped? That takes all the fun out of it! But finding paper is a last-minute hassle most people would like to be relieved of.

You can turn wrapping paper into paper money.

It may not seem like it at first, but selling wrapping paper really is a good idea. Lots of wrapping paper is sold at Christmas time. People know they're going to need piles of paper when wrapping time comes around. And *you* can bring it right to their door!

How to Do It

Plan early. This is something you'll need to do in late summer. The wrapping paper companies need orders in early, or they can't fill them all.

Make a sales kit. Look in the telephone book Yellow Pages under Paper or Paper Distributors. Call to find out which ones carry Christmas wrapping paper on large rolls. Visit the distributor and get samples of the paper they have for sale.

Pick two or three paper designs you want to sell. Make sure you pick basic patterns, the kind everyone will like. And stick with regular paper; avoid foils or tissues. If you're unsure of what to pick, ask your parents for their advice. Cut out

Your sales kit will do a lot of the selling for you.

127

samples of the papers you get and staple them together on a piece of cardboard—like the example shown here. Include a sample of paper normally sold at a discount store so you can show customers how they compare. The wrapping paper you'll buy is of much better quality than the discount store kind.

Set a price.   Check stores to find out how much wrapping paper sells for. Include the same amount of paper for the same price as in the store. (Make your comparison with one of the bigger rolls, not the skimpy ones.) That should about double the price you pay for the paper. But yours is a better buy—it's better paper, and you deliver right to the house.

Take orders.   Go around your neighborhood, to your family and friends, and to other people who might want to buy the paper. Show these people the display board you've made. Point out how much better your paper is than the discount store kind—and yours comes delivered! Get their orders for paper, and get their money if you can. The wrap comes in 18-inch and 24-inch widths. You must decide which size you are going to offer—don't give the people a choice. I'd suggest you offer only 24-inch-wide paper. Sell the paper in precut lengths the same as the length of paper sold at the discount stores.

It may sound dumb, but dress up in holiday clothing and you'll sell a lot more paper.

Santa outfit

Sales kit

And a ho, ho, ho!

Buy and cut the wrapping paper.   You'll need to order the paper rolls from the paper company long before Christmas—order in August or September. That means you need to get orders from customers before then. If you've taken deposits from people who wanted paper, make sure you tell them it'll take 6 to 8 weeks for delivery of their Christmas wrap. The rolls usually come in 833-foot lengths. Cut them to the desired length. Be sure you presell enough paper to use up all of the 833-foot rolls you buy. If you have paper left over, you won't make as much money as if you sell it all. Put a paper stay around the customer's roll of wrapping paper (the picture shows you how). Write the name, address, and amount owed on the paper stay.

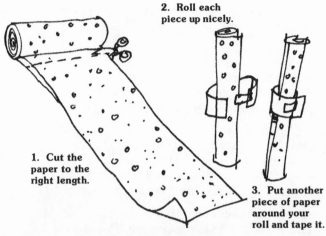

2. Roll each piece up nicely.

A few simple steps will protect the paper for your customer.

1. Cut the paper to the right length.

3. Put another piece of paper around your roll and tape it.

Deliver the wrap. Be very careful not to damage the finished rolls. No one wants to get bunged up Christmas wrap. It may help to put the rolls in large, plastic garbage bags for extra protection. Before you start delivering, make a list of the people you need to see, and draw a little route map of where you want to go. This way you can save time by delivering to all the people in one area before you move on to the rest.

Special Notes

The second year, you may want to buy the paper before you take orders. The advantage to this approach is that you can then sell the paper right before Christmas instead of at the end of the summer. If you do this, you'll need to pay for the wrap before you get any money. That means you'll need to save up to buy the wrap or you may need to borrow money from someone to pay for the rolls. Then, when you visit your customers you can leave the paper with them instead of just take orders. This way is more risky because if you don't sell all the paper you order, you still have to pay for it.

MoneyMaker!

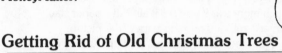

Getting Rid of Old Christmas Trees

Nothing is sadder than an old, used and worn-out Christmas tree. No one wants it anymore. And nothing is left to be done than to get it out of the house and to a safe place where it won't cause fires.

In some places, the city garbage people will haul away the trees—if that's the case where you live, you might as well stop reading and turn to the next page. But if your city doesn't provide that service, read on, my friend—there's big bucks in them thar trees!

A group of Boy Scouts once tried this project, and it was the biggest money-maker they ever did. (You can do it with just a couple of friends, if you like. All you need is a pickup and a driver.) They started by passing out a flyer just after Christmas:

"Local Scouts will haul your Christmas tree away. Reasonable rates. Call Bob at 555-2343 for arrangements. Pick-up next Saturday."

Then, on Saturday, the Scouts made their rounds. In just a few hours they'd picked up more trees than you could shake a dry branch at. It was a lot of work, but no more than they wanted.

That afternoon they took the trees to a large empty field they'd gotten permission to use. There they set the trees aflame (closely supervised, of course), and, when everything had died down, had a fun weenie roast. (Some areas wouldn't permit open fires like this, so be sure to check first.)

And here's the true measure of the success of their project: the next year they did it again!

Christmas Ornaments and Wreaths

Making ornaments and wreaths and selling them to people in the area

Christmas is a special time of year for just about everyone. The season gives people a good feeling. They like to make it different from any other season by giving gifts, putting up a tree, and decorating their homes.

You can make some extra cash for your own Christmas giving by helping people with their decorating plans. Two ways are by making and selling Christmas tree ornaments and wreaths to hang on the door.

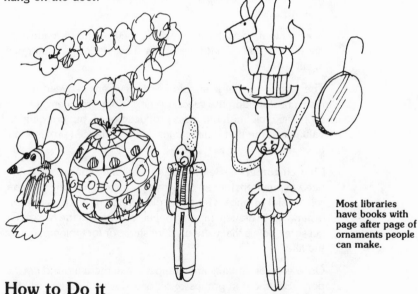

Most libraries have books with page after page of ornaments people can make.

How to Do it

Start early.   When you're waiting for Christmas, it seems to take forever before it arrives. But when you're working, making things in time for the season, the time really flies!

Your goal isn't Christmas Day, either. If you get things ready for then, you're too late. Instead you have to have *everything* done by about the first or second week of December. It would be ideal if all your ornaments and wreaths were made by the

131

time Thanksgiving arrives. The next week you can start selling. You'll have two, maybe three, weeks to sell the things you've made. The earlier you can get them sold the better.

If you want to get started even sooner, you can take orders for your ornaments and wreaths in October and early November. Then you'll be able to spend your time filling orders instead of making things you may not be able to sell.

Making the ornaments and wreaths.   The key to success in this business is making *attractive* ornaments and wreaths. Your best bet here is to make a visit to your library. It will almost certainly have books that will give you all the details you need to know.

Set a price.   Go to your local discount stores and find out what they charge for the items you've made. Their prices will probably be kind of low, because things they sell are mass-produced.

Now go to a specialty shop, where they sell hand-made ornaments. Check out their prices. Those prices will be quite high.

The price you charge should fall somewhere between the discount store and the specialty shop. Your ornaments will be more valuable than the mass-produced ones, but not quite as valuable as the hand-made ones that experienced professionals have made.

Find customers.   Before you can sell the ornaments, you need to put them into an attractive package. That way you can sell several at once. Get some old ornament boxes, wrap the ornaments in tissue wrapping paper, put them in the boxes. Or get some boxes that were used for shirts, or for typing paper, or the like.

Once your ornaments are wrapped, take them around door to door. Sell them in groups of six or a dozen. You can sell the wreaths at the same time.

Christmas Cards

Selling both stock and customized cards door to door

Some people send out dozens of Christmas cards every year. Where do they get them? Some of them buy them at the store. Some order them through the mail. And some buy them from people who come selling at their door.

If you select some good cards, you'll have success at selling them—especially if you go out early enough. You'll save people the hassle of trying to find cards elsewhere. And you'll make yourself the Christmas money you need for your own gift buying.

How to Do It

Start early.   People start thinking of Christmas just before Thanksgiving, although they don't want to do anything about it then. Just after Thanksgiving, though, they start to really get interested. That's the time to sell Christmas cards. Sell all you can between Thanksgiving and the first week of December. After that, it will be too late for most people to mail them.

If you want to sell cards in late November, you'll need to pick out the ones you want to sell before then. Pick out cards that a lot of people will like. Attractive pictures are important, even if the cards cost a little extra. If you're not sure of what kinds to get, talk to the people in a local greeting card store, or ask your parents.

To get cards to sell, look up "Greeting Cards—Wholesale and Manufacturers" in the Yellow Pages of your telephone book, or look for ads in women's and children's magazines. Or ask around to see what card companies your friends (or their friends) have worked with.

Go out selling.   Many people are going to want cards. Whether or not they'll want *your* cards will depend quite a bit on your approach. Here are some tips to keep in mind when you go to the door.
- Be courteous. Introduce yourself and tell them what you're up to.
- Call them by name, if you can.

- Explain why they'll probably want your cards instead of going somewhere else: it's convenient to have them brought to the door; you have good cards to choose from; your prices are comparable with what they'll find elsewhere.
- Thank them for their time.

Special Notes

Provide a mailing service.   Sometimes people would like to mail cards to friends and acquaintances, but they just don't have time. That opens the door for you to provide them another service: address and mail the cards for them.

To give people this service, have them sign each card, and then give the card to you with a list of addresses. You then address the envelope, buy and put on a stamp, and drop it in the mail. Your fee could be 10 cents a card, plus the money you spent on the stamp.

If you don't have neat handwriting, though, or if you don't know how to type, you might want to pass up this particular opportunity.

Make your own cards.   Some people are tired of store-bought cards, and they might welcome something new. The answer: sell them some good old-fashioned homemade cards, made by you! To do this, start early and make a few samples. Take the samples around and take orders. Then make the cards. You can make each card separately, or you can create one card (outline only), photocopy it, and then color each one separately. Whichever approach you use, make the card colorful—and make your art as neat and attractive as possible.

If you're not sure people are going to want your cards, you could take some manufactured cards with you too, to give the customer a choice.

MoneyMaker!

Gift Wrapping

Gift wrapping can be done year-round, especially when you have an established clientele, but the best time to get started is at Christmastime. That's when people have more presents to wrap than they know what to do with. It's not too hard to get into this business: put flyers on people's doorsteps, put notices on people's windshields, put posters on supermarket and department store windows. Tell them that you'll come to their home and wrap all their presents for them. You'll even provide the paper. At a busy time of year like Christmas, many people will welcome your help.

To get an idea of what to charge, time yourself while you wrap a few packages at home. Figure out how many average packages you wrap in an hour, figure out how much you need to make per hour to make the job worthwhile, and charge accordingly.

SuperIdea!

Find a Partner with Connections One of the best ideas in business is a *partnership*. In a partnership you get someone to help share the burden in your business. Instead of one person trying to make it work, both of you try to make it work—and then you share the proceeds in the proportions you've agreed on at the first.

The best kind of partner is *one with connections*. Here are some "connections" in a partner that will help your business work better:

Transportation. Some businesses really require a reliable source of transportation. If you need a way to get around, and you don't have one, that's a good sign you may need a partner with a car or pickup. If you join in a partnership to get access to a car, you won't be mooching off your parents all the time. (They might get tired of your business real quick if you're always asking them to take you places.)

So you won't be a moocher, ask your mom or dad if they'll be partners with you. You'll do all the work of the business, and they'll be your transportation when you need it. In return, they'll get a percentage of your income. (How much of a percentage will depend on how much running around they have to do.)

If your mom or dad can't do it, look around. People will be interested in what you're doing when they learn it can benefit them, too.

Money. Sometimes you'll need money to get a business going—and you don't have enough of your own. That's when you need a partner with money connections. Instead of borrowing from someone, make the money person your partner. You do all the work for the business and he puts in all the money. If and when the business becomes profitable, you split the profits in a way you've agreed on.

Supplies.   If you can get a partner with access to free or cheap supplies, you'll have one with important connections. We've heard of two kids who had that kind of partnership: one of them could get all sorts of cheap and free supplies from the company his dad owned. It made the kids' business run a lot better. The one kid's connections cut down their expenditures and helped them both make more profit.

Know-how.   You may have a great idea for making money, but you're not quite sure how to pull it off. You know the kid down the street has had experience in that area. So you approach him: "How about if we become partners in this business. You teach me all you know about it and I'll do most of the work. Then, when the profits come in, I'll take 60 percent for my work and you can have 40 percent for your know-how. What do you say?"

Customers.   Some prospective partners will have connections with customers. You might invite into a partnership a kid whose dad will sell in his grocery store the things you produce. Or he might have connections with the owner of a boutique. Or maybe his mom will buy everything he makes. The right connections can make the difference between a lackluster business and a booming one.

Vacation-time Home Care

Watching and caring for homes while the owners are away

When people go on vacation they need someone to take care of their home. If it's during the summer, they may need the lawn to be watered and mowed, the mail picked up, and the newspapers collected.

Vacation home care could be just the job for you. It usually doesn't take too much time and it pays well. And if you do a good job, it might lead to other money-making opportunities with the same homeowner.

How to Do it

Find customers. Start in your own neighborhood, where people know you—or at least know your house. Print up a bunch of flyers advertising your service and deliver them from house to house.

Once you've had some experience with people who know you, you can expand to helping other people. And now you'll have some *references* you can use: when you go to the new people, you can say, "If you'd like to call these people [the ones you worked for before] I think they'll tell you that I do a good job."

That will help you; people don't like to trust their homes to total strangers. They'll feel safer in leaving their home in your care if someone else vouches for you.

People get nervous when they leave their home to go on vacation. But you can help them feel better.

138

Offer a variety of services. The more things you can do for your customer, the better chance you'll have of getting hired. And the more money you can make on the job. Here are some services you can offer to do:

- gather the mail
- pick up the newspaper
- collect flyers off the doorknob and doorstep
- keep the lawn watered
- water the garden
- mow the lawn
- if it's winter, shovel the walks and driveway
- water the houseplants
- take care of the pets
- anything else that will make it look like the people are home, so they won't get robbed

Set a price. If you just pick up the mail and newspapers, you'll probably charge about a dollar or less a day. If you water the lawn, add on a charge for every time you have to do it. If you water houseplants, add on another charge. Mowing the lawn should bring a couple of bucks, or more, depending on the size of the lawn. And so on.

Before the people leave on their vacation, figure out how much you'll be doing for them and give them an overall bill, so they won't be surprised or upset when they get back. If they know in advance about what it's going to cost, they'll be more willing to pay it.

Follow through carefully. This probably doesn't need to be said, but it's so important to this job that a reminder doesn't hurt. Don't miss even one day in picking up the mail. The idea is to make outsiders think that someone's home—and outsiders won't think that if the mail isn't picked up. If you're supposed to water the lawn, find out exactly when and how much the owner wants you to do it. Then don't fail. Lawns can get brown fast in hot weather if they aren't watered on schedule. If you're supposed to shovel snow off the walks, do it first thing in the morning.

If the people will give you a key to their home, you can do an even better job. You can turn lights on and off each evening to make crooks think the people are home, and you can check on things in general. (One family got their whole house flooded because of a leaky tap and stuck drain. They had neighbors keep an eye on the outside, but not the inside.)

If you do everything just right, the people will hire you again. And they'll recommend you to their friends. Those are two keys to having a good business: getting people to hire you again, and having people spread the word about how good you are.

Special Notes

Expand to other home services. Now that you've shown the people what good work you can do, see if they'll let you do other things for them. You might be able to hire on permanently as a lawn-care person, or a snow shoveler. If you let them know you're interested in more work, and that you're willing to work hard, they'll probably be able to think of quite a few things they'd love to have help with.

SuperIdea!

Make Someone Feel Special   People like to feel good. And people like other people more when they make them feel good.

Think of the kids you like to hang around with. Most of the time you like to be around them because they make you feel like you're important to them. They make you feel worthwhile as a person. They make you feel special.

Those are the friends you're more willing to do things for. When the kid who's rude to you asks for a favor, chances are you won't want to do it. But when your good friend asks for one, you'll probably be happy to help him. Because he makes you feel good. And you want to make him feel good too.

When you try to get people to pay you for doing something or selling something, make them feel good. Make them feel like they're important, that they mean something. Make them feel special.

When people feel special, they're more likely to want to do business with you. Because you make them feel good about themselves. And that's the most important service you could ever provide.

Selling Maps

Selling a variety of maps door to door

Not too many years ago you could get a map at a service station just for the asking. If you were new to the area and didn't know your way around, well, that was okay—you could just go to a local service station and get a free map.

Then, as things got more expensive, some service stations started charging for their maps. People stopped getting them. And now it's hard to even *find* them.

People still want them, though. They still need to find their way around just as much as ever. And kids can make money by giving them what they need.

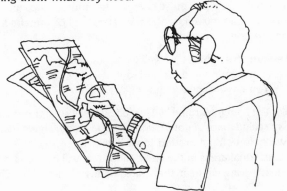

A map is one of the most useful things you can have. It makes the difference between being lost and bewildered and being confident and sure.

How to Do it

Find the maps.   You can't sell maps you don't have. That's easy enough to understand. But here's something harder: where in the world do you get them? Here are some places you can try:

- look up *Maps* in the Yellow Pages and try the places listed
- check at your state travel agency for state maps (look under the name of your state in the telephone book)
- check with your local Chamber of Commerce for city maps
- check local school supply stores
- check with bookstores
- if you have federal offices in your city, check there (look under *U.S. Government* in your telephone book)
- check with your local American Automobile Association

Of course the variety of maps you have to choose from is endless. But you'll have to limit the ones you offer to your customers. The bestsellers will probably be roadmaps for city, state, and region; and maps of recreational areas for city, state, and region.

Once you've found a source of maps, buy a few of each kind of potential bestseller—but don't get too many, until you see which ones are really going to sell the best.

Set a price. Setting the price for the maps you sell isn't difficult. Take the price you purchase them at and add on 30 or 40 percent. That will take care of your expenses (both of buying the maps and running around selling them) and will give you some well-earned profit besides. Even if you have to add that 30 or 40 percent onto the retail price, don't worry about people thinking you're charging too much. Maps aren't easy to find in many areas, and the people will be grateful for the service you're providing.

Find customers. Maps go well when sold door to door. But you can't just go to the door and say, "Hey, ya wanna buy a map?" You have to give a quick sales pitch:

"Hello, I'm Marcy Martin. I live just a few blocks over from you and I'm selling maps in your neighborhood today. I have maps that will help you get around town better, maps to show you the recreational areas in the state, maps that will help you plan your next trip anywhere in the United States. Could I show you a couple of them?"

If you can show the maps, you'll have a better chance of selling them. It will give the customer a better idea of how he could use the maps.

Special Notes

Make a neighborhood map. One map that many people would like, and that they can't get *anywhere*, is a map of the neighborhood. Neighborhood maps are nice because they help people picture better where friends and neighbors and shops are. They're also useful to copy and give out to people who are coming to visit—with the map the visitor will know exactly how to get to the house.

The only way people will get such a map is if you draw it for them. If you get a hundred customers for your neighborhood map, you don't have to draw them all, of course. Just make one clear copy, then you can have the others photocopied or printed up.

The first step to making up a neighborhood map is deciding how much area you're going to cover. If you live in a subdivision or apartment complex, that might automatically suggest how big your map area will be. Otherwise, you'll just have to pick a size area you think would work well. Some neighborhood maps show the houses and stores for a three-block-square area; others show ten square blocks.

Include on your map all kinds of interesting details— the names of the people who live in each house, what their phone number is (unless it's unlisted), how many children there are (with ages and names), and things like that.

Whenever you make a map, you'll want to be sure it's accurate. Here's the best way to draw an accurate map:

First, draw a rough outline of the map on regular paper. Then get some graph paper (the kind that's covered with little squares) and transfer your drawing to it. Make all the houses on the map about the same size as each other— maybe you'll want to use one or two squares on the paper for each house. Also make all city blocks the same as each other.

Once you have the map on the graph paper all ready, get some tracing paper and draw the map onto it— with a *dark* pen or pencil. Write in the details you want to include, and take it to the photocopier. You'll be in business!

Make a treasure map.   This is another fun map people will like. Buy a treasure, like a transistor radio or a neat book or a batch of candy, and hide it in a good, safe place. Then make a complicated map of how to find it, and sell the map to kids in the area. Tell the kids what the treasure is, so they'll know if they want to participate or not. Also tell them you'll post the name of the winner, and the date he or she found the treasure, at a central location in the area.

Make a "neat stuff" map.   Talk to people in the area and find out where all the neat stuff is. You'll know where a lot of it is, and other people can tell you more. Find out where the best restaurants are, the best stores, the best places to visit, the most unique shops, the best parks, and so on. Put them all on your map.

Once you have your maps made, you can sell them the same way you do the other maps. If you want to make even more money, have a nearby business sponsor you. Put the business name on the map as an advertisement and have them pay for all the maps. Then you can just distribute the maps but not charge customers for the map. Or have the business pay just for the printing and you can charge the customers for the map. With a "neat stuff" map, the businesses you recommend might be willing to sell the maps for you.

MoneyMaker!

Backyard Carnival

A friend shares an experience common to many of us: "One of my first experiences with making money was a backyard carnival. My brothers, the neighborhood boys, and I all got together and did all kinds of things to amuse our parents and the other neighbor kids. Unfortunately we didn't charge nearly enough and ended up with only $1 to split between five of us at the end of the day. (It didn't help that we lived in a farming area, with only six houses on our whole street!)"

Backyard carnivals can be a fun way to earn extra cash—or they can be an ambitious plan that backfires. If you live in an area where there are lots of kids, you might be able to have a successful day. But plan carefully!

On a sleepy summer day kids (and sometimes parents) are looking for something to do. You can give them that something with your backyard carnival—and make some money in the process.

To put together a good backyard carnival, make a detailed plan of what you want to do. You should have plenty of games, like ring-toss and throw-the-dart-at-the-balloon, with prizes. You should have special attractions, like a magic show or a short play. You can have a lottery or raffle. You can have bingo. You can even have a flea market at the same time. And don't forget: lots of food and goodies to sell!

A backyard carnival is a job for several kids working together, of course. The more activities you can have, the more people will be interested in coming, the longer they'll stay, and the more money they'll spend. The best way to be successful is to divide up the work. One person can be in charge of food, one in charge of putting together booths or tables, one in charge of advertising, and so forth.

The best way to find out how to do a backyard carnival is to talk to people who have had experience in that sort of thing. You may not be able to find anyone in your area who has put on a carnival, but you probably can find someone who has worked in a bazaar or community fair. They'll be able to give you some excellent suggestions.

Selling Calendars

Selling copies of the upcoming year's calendar door to door

Many people have at least two calendars in their houses every year, as well as one at work. And every year they have to replace them.

If someone came to the door selling calendars during December and early January, it would save people a lot of trouble. And bring the salesperson some extra cash.

Pick your time to sell the calendars very carefully—do it in mid-December to mid-January for the best sales.

How to Do It

Get a source of calendars. The first step is to get some calendars to sell. There are two possibilities. One is to go to local bookstores or office-supply stores and arrange to sell some of their calendars on commission. That means that for every calendar you sell, you get 10 or 20 percent of the selling price to keep.

Another approach is to go directly to the wholesale distributor. Find out who sends the calendars to the local stores. It will probably be a book or magazine distributor. See if you can make an arrangement with them to sell calendars. They'll give them to you cheaper than the store can—but you'll have to buy a batch at a time.

There are basically two kinds of calendars: cutesy or artsy ones, that people buy because they like the way they look; and functional ones, that people buy to tell them what day it is, or to

146

write appointments or messages on. Cutesy or artsy ones usually cost more, and there's a wider variety of them. I'd recommend you try to sell the other kind, the functional ones. They won't cost as much, and people won't care as much how they look. That way you won't have to offer such a big variety. Maybe you can sell two kinds: a kind with nature pictures, and a kind without any pictures at all.

Set a price. If you sell for a local store, they'll tell you the price to sell the calendars for. But if you buy your own calendars from a distributor, you'll have to set your own price. Ask the distributor how much stores usually add on to the price. Then add on just a bit less than they do.

Try selling large-size calendars to offices—those can be big sellers.

Find customers. Customers for calendars are everywhere. Start with your own family—your parents and grandparents, aunts and uncles. Maybe your brother and sister will want to have their own calendar for their room. Talk to your parents' friends. Ask your mom or dad if you can sell calendars to people where they work. And every time you sell a calendar, ask the customer to spread the word that you have great calendars at a price that can't be beat!

After you've tried those places, start going door to door. Introduce yourself and tell the customer what you have. "Hello, I'm Robin Wilson. I live a couple of blocks over, and I'm selling calendars for a good price. I have a couple of kinds to choose from. Can I show them to you?"

Take good care of the calendars you're selling. No one wants a cruddy calendar!

Special Notes

Sell Christmas items. If you sell calendars before Christmas, you might as well sell a Christmas item or two at the same time. That will give you more mileage per visit. You can sell Christmas cards, Christmas wreaths, ornaments, and so forth. You might make arrangements to come back after they get a tree and attach a stand to it. But don't try to sell too much at one visit—that could irritate some prospective buyers. For details on selling Christmas items, see the sections on Christmas in this book.

MoneyMaker!

Make a Neighborhood Calendar

One surefire way to sell calendars is to make your own. Start by making up a sheet with dark lines on it, forming boxes for the days of the month. Take the sheet to a copy machine and make twelve copies of it. Take your copied sheets back home again and write in the name of a month on the top of each sheet, with the days of the month in the boxes where they belong. (Be sure to write the days in the way they'll be *next* year.)

Next, line up twelve neighborhood kids to help you. They will all get a little money, plus they will get the glory of having their artwork on a calendar for a month. Get each of the kids to draw a picture, outline only, in heavy black. Make sure the kids artwork sheets, combined with your month sheets, come to 8 ½ inches by 14 inches in size.

Now take your twelve month sheets back to the copier, along with the pictures the neighborhood kids drew. Match up a picture to each month sheet, the picture on top of the month, and run off a few dozen copies of each, on legal-sized (8 ½ inches by 14 inches) paper.

You now have your basic calendar. But don't put it together yet. Have each of your artists color his picture on all the copies. It will take awhile, but it will be worth it for him when the calendars sell.

When all the calendars are colored, make a cover sheet to go on top, giving the year and a description of the calendar. It might say: "1986—Neighborhood Kids' Calendar." Make a bunch of copies of the cover sheet, then put it with the calendars and staple each one firmly on the top, with at least three staples.

You've gone to a lot of work and haven't made a thing yet. But here's where the payoff comes. Give a batch of calendars to each of the kids and have them sell them for $3 or so. They can sell to parents, brothers and sisters, grandparents, and older friends. The sales pitch should always include the important fact that "I did March!" Let the other kids keep half or one-third of the money they make. They should give you the rest. Be sure to keep careful track of who takes how many calendars.

While the other kids are selling to relatives, you take the calendars around the neighborhood. Explain how the calendar was made, and name a few of the artists that the people would know. A good number of neighbors will probably be interested in buying a calendar. On the calendars *you* sell, you get to keep the whole amount.

SuperIdea!

Be Unique   One of the best things a businessperson can do is to be unique. It's being different that sells, whether you're trying to get someone to buy a product or use your services.

Think about the advertisements you remember, on TV or billboards. Why do you remember them? Because they were different from all the others. And you want to get that same difference going for your business.

Start by picking a company name that will help people remember what your business is. Ways to do that:

- Put your name in the company name. Ronny's Cleaning Service works better than Cleaning Service. It even works better than Ron's Cleaning Service.
- Make the name into a pun or a rhyme, or have the words in your business name all start with the same letter. For instance, there's a clothes store in my city called Bud's Duds. A store that specializes in pants is called Mad Man Magee's. Those names are unique—people remember them. And the name you choose should do the same.
- Have a personal trademark that makes you different. One kid always wears the same weird hat when he works. He looks kind of funny in it—and he knows it—but he doesn't mind. He knows it makes people remember him.

Have a special twist to your service that people will remember. Maybe you could have business cards printed up that say: "This window cleaned by Wendy's Windowers," or "Apples from EverRed Apple Company." Put the card by your work and people will remember.

Wear a special T-shirt that will advertise the thing you do. Make it neat—make it unique!

Delivering Leaflets and Handbills

Delivering printed advertising and flyers door to door

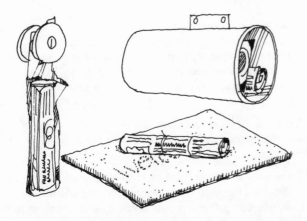

Every time you see a leaflet hung on a doorknob, you can bet that someone made some money that day. Maybe next time it will be you!

In some areas, people find a new batch of handbills or coupons on the doorknob nearly every week. Those kinds of advertising materials are very useful for local merchants—they tell the people in the area who's offering what services, and what kinds of special deals are available.

The amount that advertisers pay for delivery of handbills isn't very high, when you look at the payment for each handbill. But add it all up together and a person will have himself some needed extra cash. And businesses are often in the market for new people to deliver.

How to Do It

Find a distributor. Start by contacting some of the local advertising agencies. They often need someone to distribute printed materials. And, since they're working for several businesses at once, they'll sometimes pay better than a single business will.

If you've contacted all the advertising agencies in your area, and you still want more work, you can start by contacting some of the individual stores. The bigger ones will be more likely to be interested in having advertising distributed. Be sure to talk to the manager—he's the one who makes the decisions, and he might have other work for you, too.

A final place to check is with political candidates. During election years they often need to have material distributed. You can help them out, and yourself too, by going door to door for them.

Make an agreement.   If the store or advertiser uses handbills a lot, they'll have a set price they'll want to pay you. If the store doesn't do it often, they may be unsure what to pay. You can make suggestions, recommending a fair wage. But whatever you do, make sure you agree in advance how much you'll be paid.

The price for handbills is usually set by the *number of pieces* you distribute. That pays you to work faster, and to try to get more handed out.

Sometimes a company will have so many handbills or leaflets to distribute that they won't want to hire just one person. In that case, you can gather a group of friends and hire them to help you.

MoneyMaker!

Outdoor Painting

If you really want to get ambitious, and if you have some experience, you can get into house painting, both inside and out. But that takes a fair amount of expertise. Here's another way you can do painting for pay, a way that doesn't require so much experience: try painting fences, sheds, garages, patio furniture. All outdoor wood needs to be repainted from time to time, and it's a job that most people would just as soon put off. Sometimes they'll have the paint you need; other times you'll need to get it for them. If you have to pick up the paint, increase the price of the job accordingly. Your overall charge can be by the hour or by the job.

Deliver the materials. Delivering handbills is just as important as any other job. That means you need to hand them out as agreed—at the proper time and to the proper places. A handbill announcing a sale on Saturday isn't going to do much good if the people don't get it until Saturday morning.

Sometimes kids are tempted to do a sloppy job passing out handbills. A kid in our area once hid a few hundred in a culvert under a road—then took the money as though he'd distributed them from door to door. People like that make it hard for everyone else. (That kind of approach to work doesn't help a person feel very good about himself. And when the handbills were finally found, you can imagine what it did to the kid's reputation.)

Special Notes

Set up a regular schedule. The best job is one that allows you to do it over and over again. That's when you start to make money on a regular schedule, instead of just hit and miss.

When you're making arrangements with the advertiser (either the agency or the store or the political person), tell them you'd like to deliver materials for them regularly. Let them know that you'll be available to do it every week, if they need someone that often. Then follow up and contact them again. "I did a good job for you last time. Do you have some more for me to distribute this time?" Pretty soon you'll be one of their "regular employees"!

Some kids have had success in going to local stores, finding out what sales they have going on, and making their own handbills of the sales. Then they get the store manager to pay them for distributing to the area.

153

MoneyMaker!

Subscription Service

You've heard of magazine subscriptions—the person gets the magazine every month without having to buy it each time at the newsstand. You've also heard of the old milk route, where the milkman delivers the milk right to your doorstep a couple of times a week.

A subscription service works the same way. Here's how:
- Select a few grocery items that people are always running out of. Good ones to select are bread, milk, eggs, cheese, and maybe fruit.
- Distribute a flyer or go door to door lining up a list of people who would like a weekly delivery of some of those items.
- Charge your "subscribers" the cost of the items they need, plus 10 percent for your delivery.
- Set up a standard day and time when you'll make your delivery of the requested items. The delivery will be the same every week unless the subscriber notifies you otherwise.

Framing Service
for Kids' Artwork

Framing kids' artwork for their parents to hang

A gradeschooler brings home a magnificent drawing. It's of a lion in the jungle—and his folks have never seen such a fine lion. Or, for that matter, such a fine jungle. They look at the drawing for a minute, say, "We've got to save this one!" and then set it aside and forget it exists.

It's not that the mom and dad don't really love the picture, because they do. The problem is that they don't have a good way to display it. So it gets filed away and forgotten.

You can help them out by giving them a way to display the artwork.

How to Do It

Buy some frames. Go to a discount store or a frame shop and buy a bunch of inexpensive, but attractive, frames. You may want to buy some that aren't stained and put the stain on yourself. That will be cheaper but will take more time. Be careful of the size you pick—not too large, and not too small. A frame for an 8 inch by 10 inch picture is probably best. That will hold a standard size of paper.

Some frames have *mats* in them. Mats are colored cardboard borders, and they're nice for dressing up a picture. If you can get a frame with a mat, do so. That will make the picture you put inside look better than ever.

Set a price. Add together the price of the frame, the price of the stain (if any), and the cost of your time. Include *all* the time you put into the project: buying frames, staining them, finding customers, and putting the art with the frames. Those figures added together should give you the price you'll charge your customers. But make sure it's fair, or no one will want to buy.

Find customers. Find a neighborhood that has a lot of younger kids and go door to door. Talk to one of the parents and explain your service. Tell them, "You probably have some favorite pieces of art by your child, but don't have a way to display them. It would be neat to have some of those artworks

hanging on the wall in a frame—and I can help you do it."
Show them a sample frame, with a kid's picture in it, so they
can see how attractive it looks. Then ask if they can give you
some pictures to take home today, so you can frame them.

Put the drawing with the frame. It's not difficult to put the
art with the frame, but be careful that you don't ruin the art.
First attach the art to a thin cardboard backing, to keep it stiff.
You can put it on with scotch tape on the corners. Try not to
put any tape over the drawing itself, though sometimes you
won't have any choice, since the drawing will cover the entire
sheet of paper.

Your next step is to put the mat over the drawing. Then put the
glass into the frame and the picture and the mat in behind it.
Finally, use the staples that came with the frame to make sure
the picture is secure.

The picture will give you an overview of how everything fits
together.

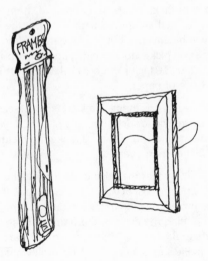

When a picture is
framed, it
becomes more
enjoyable to look
at than it ever was
before.

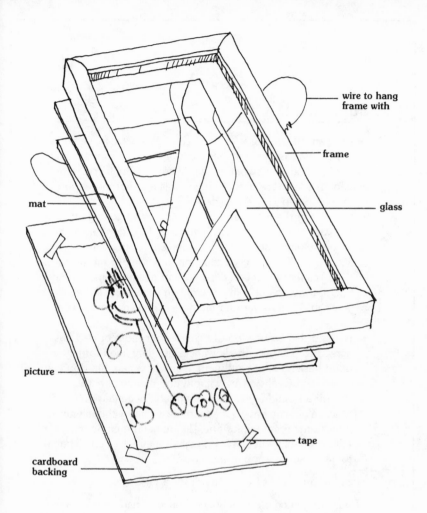

wire to hang
frame with

frame

mat

glass

picture

tape

cardboard
backing

SuperIdea!

Getting an Allowance   You don't always have to leave home to make extra cash. Sometimes the best source of funds is your own folks. You don't want to beg, of course. But if you're not getting an allowance now, or if you'd like to get more, you might be able to. Try these ideas:

- Get one in the first place. Some kids aren't getting an allowance to start with. It isn't that their folks don't have the money (sometimes!) — they just haven't ever given an allowance. If this is your situation, talk to your mom and dad. Tell them that you'd like to start making some money, and the way to get going is to get an allowance. If they like, you can do more around the house in exchange for the money.
- Remind dad so he won't forget. If your mom or dad has agreed to pay you an allowance, but they keep forgetting, don't hesitate to remind them. Don't be a nag, but don't let weeks and weeks go by without any money either.
- Ask for a raise. Maybe the amount you're getting isn't very much. You may have gone for quite a while without a raise. If that's the case, ask for one. (If you get turned down, your folks probably don't have enough money. Then you'll have to get busy on a job in this book.)

Here are a couple of ways to ask for a raise:

"Dad, I'm getting older now and I haven't had an allowance raise for quite a while. Do you think I could have one now?"

"Mom, I'd like to get more in allowance — and if you're willing, I'll agree to do something extra for it."

That second approach might work best. Often the best way to get more money is to provide more services. This is as true with allowances as it is with anything else. To get more allowance, offer to do something you haven't been doing:

- wash the dishes three nights a week
- vacuum the carpets every Saturday morning

- mow the lawn
- shovel the snow off the driveway or walks
- babysit little brothers or sisters
- do a load of laundry every week
- clean the bathrooms once a week
- rake the leaves in the yard

MoneyMaker!

Raising and Selling Houseplants

Go to the discount store or the nursery and look at the plants they have for sale. You'll notice that there's a wide variety of sizes—and prices. A plant that may cost 50 cents when it's little may cost $5 when it's bigger. And the only difference between the two is some time and a little care.

Set up your houseplant business by buying a bunch of those little plants. The people at the nursery can tell you which are people's favorites, and which are easiest for people to take care of. Take your plants home and give them the care they need. (Ask the nursery people for instructions on how much sun or shade they'll need, and how much water.) Let them grow. You may need to transplant them when they're bigger. (Again, you'll want to check with an expert or find out the proper procedure in a gardening book.)

You may also want to try to start easy plants from seed. The gardening book or nursery expert can help you know which ones to try.

When you're ready to sell, put your plants in fancy pots and increase the price accordingly. Try a variety of selling methods to make your business most profitable.

Selling Fruit and Vegetables

Selling fresh farm produce, in season, to homes and at football games

Nothing's better than fresh fruit or vegetables. When it's peach season, fresh peaches are one of the finest things on the planet. A lot of people just can't get enough.

Kids can help fill that gap. When peach time comes around, fresh peaches for sale will go like gangbusters. When apple time arrives, fresh apples will sell faster than you can pick them!

How to Do It

Find a source of fruit or vegetables.   Maybe you have a big garden in your backyard that will supply you with all the vegetables you can sell. Or maybe you have a little orchard.

If you do, great. You're better off than we are!

People who don't have their own fruit or vegetables can do one of three things:

1. Make arrangements with a neighbor who grows fruit and vegetables. Agree to pick and sell his crop and, in exchange, give him a third of the proceeds. Or pick it in exchange for mowing the lawn and keep all the proceeds for yourself.

2. Make arrangements with a farmer to sell some of his produce. You may be able to split the profits with him, or you may need to pay him a wholesale price right up front.

3. Go to a local produce distributor and buy in bulk from him. Then you'll need to package it in your own boxes or bags to sell to your customers. The distributor may be able to sell you those boxes or bags, too.

Set a price.   Go to a couple of your local supermarkets and find out what they're charging for fruit and vegetables. Check with fruit stands, or farmers' markets in your area. You can charge competitive prices. If you can tell your customers that you've compared prices and yours is definitely the lowest, they'll be more willing to buy from you.

Take this test: Which of these batches of fruit will sell better—the nice one or the messy one?

Apples are always a big seller.

Find customers. There are two ways to find customers for fresh fruit and vegetables. Both work well, depending on what area you're in. The first is to go door to door. One man tried this approach with some others in a club he belonged to, and it worked very well. They were selling apples by the bushel, and they offered people at the door an apple to try, for free. The apples were crisp and cold and juicy, and just about everybody wanted more. They were willing to buy a bushel at once.

Another way to find customers for fresh fruits and vegetables is to set up a roadside stand. Make a big sign to put up by the side of the road, and then just wait for the customers to drive by. Be sure to pick a busy road—but pick a place where people can pull their cars off onto the side without any danger. (And be sure this is legal in your area.)

161

Special Notes

Sell at football games.   Football means fall—and fall means apples. When people go to football games, whether they're junior high, high school, college, or pro, they're wanting something to eat. What could be better than a cold, juicy apple?

A good place to sell the apples, if you can get permission, is just outside the ticket gate. Set up a big sign where you're sure to be seen and call out what you're up to: "Apples! Apples! Twenty cents each!" Do all you can to get people to see and hear you.

Another place to sell, after the game has started, is out in the stands. Carry a few apples with you and walk around the stadium, calling out what you're doing. But don't get into anybody's way—especially during the big play of the game. The tunnels under the stadium, which lead to the restrooms and concession stands are also good places to set up shop, if the stadium people will let you. You may have to give them a percentage of what you earn—but it will probably be worth it anyway.

It would help if you had a few dollars in change handy. And a pouch to hold it in—and to hold the money you'll be making!

SuperIdea!

Be Professional When Roger was in junior high, he always had more money than he knew what to do with. No, he didn't get it from his folks. They didn't have much to spare. If Roger wanted to have some spending money he had to earn it all himself.

Roger wasn't any smarter than anybody else. He didn't have any skills his friends didn't have. But he was rolling in dough while the rest of the kids could barely scrape up a quarter for a video game.

What made the difference between Roger and his friends was one thing: *he acted professional.* When he went to sell something to someone, he looked the part. When he wanted to perform a service for them, he looked like he could do it. It didn't matter that he was "just a kid." He acted like he knew what he was doing; he looked like he knew what he was doing—and then he did it!

A friend of ours recently told us this experience: "There's a service station near me that I go to pretty frequently. Usually when I stop to get gas I'm wearing jeans and a T-shirt, or something else just as casual. Not long ago I stopped by wearing a three-piece suit. You wouldn't believe the difference in how they treated me. When I was casual, they treated me casually—I was just another customer. But when I was dressed up, suddenly I was an Important Customer!"

Look like what you want to be. Act like what you want to be. Then other people will find it much easier to believe you are that thing.

Babysitting

Watching little kids while their folks are away

Parents love their kids a lot. But even loving parents need a break. They need the chance to go out and do adult things, without worrying about their baby crying or their five-year-old running off after something that's caught his fancy.

A lot of you reading this book have probably done babysitting before. But you can do it on an even bigger scale than you've done it before. Kids who go after the job can really turn it into a regular business.

Little kids come in all shapes and sizes. But they're special and need great care.

How to Do it

Find customers.   People who want babysitting services are all over—and so is your competition. You can make the difference by advertising. Try some of these ideas:

- ask your parents to tell their friends you'd like to babysit
- pass out a flyer around your neighborhood or apartment house
- put up a notice on a bulletin board in Laundromats or supermarkets
- put a notice in your church newsletter or a women's group newsletter

Set a price.   Several things combine to determine how much you can charge for babysitting. Will you have to dress the kids for bed and put them there? Will you have to prepare a meal and feed the kids? How many kids will there be? Do any of the kids require special care?

Check around your area to find out what the going rate is. Be sure to put your rate on your flyer and in your notices. When you get new customers, don't be shy about telling them what your rates are. Your babysitting is a business, and you should treat it that way.

Make a schedule.   The best way to make money babysitting is to get on a regular schedule. A schedule is like going steady: you always know you're going to be needed on a particular night. You may agree with the parents to babysit every Friday night beginning at 6:30, for example. If you can get two or three customers like that, you'll really be in business.

A Success Story

A friend tells this story about when he moved into a new area: "When my wife and I moved into a new community, we didn't know who to get for a babysitter. We checked around and got some referrals. Then we tried some of the kids out. The first one was very messy. When she got our kids ready for bed, she left their clothes all over the house.

"The second one came to our house and seemed more interested in looking at the TV than listening to our instructions. Obviously, we didn't have a lot of confidence in leaving our children with him!

"The third babysitter turned out to be a jewel. She kept things neat and clean, she got the kids to bed on time—she even washed the dishes for us! We were so pleased that we paid her a bonus, and we used her over and over again. Her conscientiousness made her worth the extra money we paid her."

Get repeat business. There are two basic ways to get repeat babysitting business:

1. Do your job in a way that will make the parents want to have you back.

2. Do your job in a way that will make the kids want to have you back.

If you can keep the kids happy and keep the house in good order, you'll keep the parents happy. That means you don't let the kids make messes. If they do, you get them cleaned up. And it also means that you don't just come to the house, plop down in front of the TV, and waste your time away till the parents come back.

Kids love to be played with and read to. Bring a sack full of fun things to do: pictures to draw, pages to color, clothes to dress up in, sacks to make into masks, storybooks to read together, and so on. Keep the kids busy having fun and they won't have time to give you trouble. And they'll want you to come back again next time.

Take notes about where the parents will be and of any instructions they have to give. That will impress them and help them feel confident about your ability.

Special Notes

Observe the rules of babysitting. There are some basic rules every babysitter should obey. Obeying them will build the sitting business and make things go better. Here are a few to keep in mind:

166

- Put the kids to bed on time.
- Don't just entertain yourself with the TV—spend your time *with* the kids.
- When the parents give instructions, listen carefully.
- Make sure the parents tell you where they're going, how they can be reached in an emergency, and when they'll be back.
- Don't eat anything unless the parents invite you to. If you take food without permission, that's stealing.
- Don't talk on the telephone with friends.
- If someone calls, don't tell them you're alone at the house with younger kids. Don't tell them you're the babysitter. Just say, "Mr. Collins can't come to the phone right now. May I take a message?"
- Give the phone number of where you'll be to your parents, so they can call if they need to.
- If your parents won't be around for you to ask advice, if needed, have them suggest someone else you can call.
- Don't let the kids mess up the house. Let the parents come home to a house that's at least as clean as the one they left.
- Don't have friends over.
- If the parents are going to be gone until quite late, ask if it's okay for you to go to sleep after the kids are in bed.
- Don't leave the house, unless it's on fire. Then be sure to take the kids with you.
- Keep emergency telephone numbers handy, just in case.

A Success Story

Being alert can make a world of difference when you're tending kids. One girl was able to save the day by being on her toes. One of the little boys she was babysitting had to go up to the bathroom. The babysitter noticed the little boy seemed to be up there a long time. so she went up to check.

Somehow someone had left the water in the bathtub—and the little boy had climbed in to play. Now he was lying face-down in the water.

The babysitter grabbed him out and quickly gave him mouth-to-mouth resuscitation, which she had learned in a community first-aid class. The boy was quickly revived.

But she didn't leave it at that. She had made sure that the parents gave her a phone number where they could be reached, and now she called the number. They hurried home and took the boy to the hospital emergency room to make sure everything was okay.

Everything *was* okay—thanks to this babysitter's alertness and quick thinking.

Do something extra.   After the kids are in bed, take a quick look around the living room, family room, and kitchen areas. If they need to be tidied up, take the time to do it. If there are dishes to be done, do them. The parents may not pay you extra for your work (then again, they may), but you *can* be sure they'll want to ask you back again. And you'll feel a lot better about your evening, too,

Expand to shut-in sitting.   If you want your business to grow, you can expand to other services. For instance, many people have their elderly parents living with them—parents who can't go anywhere because they've got some kind of illness. You can hire on to sit with those parents. You can chat with them about your life and theirs—they'll love it and so will you. Or you can read to them. If they're unable to talk, you may just want to sit beside them to keep them company. You can read to yourself in those cases.

Saturday sitting.   A variation of regular babysitting is to set up a Saturday service. Pass flyers around your neighborhood telling the people to bring their kids to your house at a certain time on Saturday. (Be sure to get your parents' permission first! And be sure to clean up after the babysitting session is over.)

In your flyer, tell your prospective customers the hours you'll be sitting and the amount you'll charge per kid per hour. Tell them the activities you'll be doing. (Plan a full day of fun activities for the kids.) And tell them to be sure to call you in advance, so you'll know how many kids to plan for. If quite a few people are interested, you may need to find a friend or two to help you with all the kids.

Some times when this kind of service might work best:
- when parents want to get away from the kids to do some Christmas shopping
- when the parents want to go to the Saturday matinee
- when the parents just want a quiet Saturday morning at home
- when lots of people will be going to an important local football game

You might want to include some of those reasons in your flyer, just to tempt the parents to take you up on your offer.

A Success Story

A boy in our area has a thriving babysitting business. He always has more work than he can handle. In fact, some months he has to keep an appointment calendar to keep track of all the babysitting he's agreed to do. And he always commands top rates for his work. His secret: "I like to play with the kids. When I'm babysitting, I don't worry about what's on TV—instead I take the chance to spend some fun time with the children I'm babysitting. Because of that the kids like me and always ask their parents to have me back."

MoneyMaker!

Quickie Sitting Service.

Sometimes mom or dad has to take off for just a few minutes, to run to the store or do some other kind of errand. They hesitate to call a babysitter—they don't want to bother them for a half-hour job. But at the same time they don't want to drag the kids all over the store.

Advertise yourself as providing a Quickie Babysitting Service, and you'll be able to help out those parents. When they know you're willing and ready to come over on the spur of the moment, even if it's just for a twenty-minute job, they'll take you up on the offer. (Stick to your own neighborhood in offering this service. If you try to go too far, a quick job won't pay for itself.)

And you'll enjoy two advantages: you'll probably be paid more per minute on a short job than you are on a long job. And the parents will also be more likely to call you when they need a babysitter for all evening.

MoneyMaker!

Decorating Cakes

The ability to decorate a cake is a real skill, and those who can do it well are paid good money for their work. There's no reason why a younger person, especially someone with a little artistic ability, couldn't learn how to do a good decorating job.

Step 1: Go to the local bakery and ask if you can watch the decorator at work.

Step 2: If your community education services have a cake decorating class, take one. Also check your library for books that will help.

Step 3: Get some cake decorating tubes and tips and *practice*. You can practice over and over on the same cake—simply wipe off the frosting and try again. Or you can practice on a piece of cardboard.

Step 4: Learn how to bake a good cake.

Step 5: When you're good at cake baking and decorating, advertise your services. Notices in supermarket windows and on bulletin boards are good places to start. When you hear someone's having a birthday, offer to supply a decorated cake. Charge a little less than the bakery does.

Dried Flowers

Picking, drying, and selling flowers

Stop by a specialty shop or a florist and see how much dried flowers cost. Unless you're a millionaire, you might be surprised at how expensive they are. A large part of that cost is pure profit to the people involved. Why shouldn't you get some of those profits yourself, by setting up a dried flower business?

Dried flower arrangements are popular in all parts of the country.

How to Do It

Find the flowers.   Before you can dry and sell the flowers you have to find some! That's simple enough to say—and hopefully it will be simple enough to do, too! Here are some places to try:

- grow some in your own yard
- grow some in a window box
- get some from neighbors who have too many
- pick up the cut-offs and cast-offs of local florists (they have plenty they just throw away)
- find a vacant lot that has some
- check along country roads near your home
- go into the woods and grassy hillsides (with permission from the owners)

Know what to look for. The best way to know what flowers and plants to look for is to get a field guide to plants in your area. The guide will describe the plants and will give pictures of what they look like.

The best plants and wild flowers for drying include the following:

daisy	yarrow	tansy
goldenrod	butterfly weed	milkweed
pearly everlasting	dock	sumac
thistle	cattail	bittersweet
Queen Anne's lace	mullein	teasel

grains:

barley	oats	rye
corn	rice	wheat
millet		

tree seed pods:

eucalyptus	sycamore	magnolia
locust	sweet gum	

garden-seed pods:

yucca	poppy	peony
lily	perennial sweet pea	honesty
columbine		

The best garden flowers for drying:

acacia	snapdragon	lilac
China Aster	delphinium	narcissus
bells of Ireland	marigolds	tulip
celosia	strawflowers	peony
rose	baby's-breath	pansy
cosmos	heather	wandflower
zinnia	hydrangea	

Learn to dry the plants and flowers. There's a knack to drying flowers, and doing it right can make the difference between a successful business and a failure. Most flowers take a week or more to dry properly—and they take good space to do it in. It would take a big chapter in a book to completely describe how to dry flowers. The best thing to do is to go to the library and see what they have.

Here are some books you might check for:
The Art of Drying Plants and Flowers, by Mabel Squires
Get Started in Dried Flower Craft, by B. Amlick
ABC of Flower Arranging, by Julia Clements
How to Dry Flowers the Easy Way, by Audrey Bugbee
Flowercraft, by Eunice Svinicki
Keeping the Plants You Pick, by Laura Foster
Flowers Are for Keeping, by Joella Cramblic and JoAnn Loebel
The Complete Book of Flower Preservation, by Geneal Condon

Learn to package the flowers. The better your flowers look, the better chance you'll have of selling them. It's a good idea to put them together in attractive packages, both to preserve them better and to make them more appealing to your customers.

An arrangement that's carefully done will sell a lot better than one that's not so attractive, even though the flowers might look the same on both.

Find customers. People who want to buy dried flowers are all over. And if you can sell them cheaper than the craft shop can, you'll really be in business. Start by contacting your neighbors. Show them the flowers you've dried and give them a sales pitch. Tell them how your price compares with the price of the stores.

If you have enough flowers, you may also want to try selling to florists and craft and specialty shops. Your flowers will need to be top quality—but that's how you'll want them to be anyway!

Special Notes

Choose the best flowers. Some flowers are popular dried, and some aren't. It's important that you pick the ones that will sell best. Some of the flowers you'll sell are more like weeds—and some of those will bring the highest price! One good way to pick the best flowers is to go to a local boutique and see what kinds they're selling—and for how much.

173

A Reminder Person

Reminding busy people of dates they don't want to forget

Busy people have a lot of important dates to remember—sometimes more than the rest of us. But they're often so busy that they can't always remember them all.

But that's okay. Because they can hire a reminder person to help them remember.

How to Do It

Find customers. I'd suggest you start finding customers by contacting busy people you know. With your folks' permission, contact people they work with—maybe their boss, or his boss.

Contact your clergyman to see if he needs your service—or if he knows someone who does.

Put a notice on bulletin boards of office buildings.

Put ads in local papers.

Whenever you talk to someone about your business, whether he needs you or not, ask if he knows someone else who would be interested. That way your business will grow and grow.

Set a price. Probably the best way to charge for being a reminder person is by the reminder: *each time* you remind the person, charge 25 cents or 50 cents for the service. The reminder can be a phone call or a note in the mail, whichever your customer prefers. And ask the customer how far in advance he wants to be reminded: the same day, the day before, the week before, or whatever. It would be sad for you to remind him only to have him forget again!

Create a calendar. Fix yourself up a calendar that has the following information on it:
- The date you need to remind the customer of.
- Who the customer is.
- When he needs to be reminded.
- What the event is.
- How the customer wants you to remind him.

Special Notes

Buy the presents or supplies.   When a person is too busy to
remember important dates, sometimes he's too busy to
prepare for them. Suppose he has a wedding anniversary
coming up—and you're going to remind him to be sure he
doesn't forget. Also offer to buy a gift for him to give his wife.
He tells you what to buy and gives you the money. You buy
the gift, and charge him something for the service—say 5 or 10
percent of the cost of the gift.

You can do the same thing if he needs to be reminded of an
important business meeting—maybe you can buy him some
pencils and pads of paper for it, or maybe you can pick up
some valuable papers he needs.

That way you can turn one business into two!

SuperIdea!

Keeping Records Keeping good records of your business will be one of the best ideas you'll ever try. Sometimes it can even make the difference between success and failure.

The first thing to do is get a notebook to keep your records in. Draw in lines to make several columns. You'll probably want to make a page for every month. What you want to keep a record of is everything you spend money on, and everything you make money on.

Your notebook might look like this:

January

Expenses		Income	
Item	Amount	Source	Amount

Under expenses, write on the left side of the column what you spent the money on. On the right side of the column, put the amount you spent. At the end of the month, add up all the figures and put the total at the bottom.

Under income, write on the left side of the column what you did to make the money. On the right side, write the amount you made. Total these figures up at the end of the month, too.

You may also want to make a column to show the dates of your expenditures and income.

You'll be able to tell how well you're doing by the end of the first month. Compare what you spent with what you made. If you made more, your business is going well. If you spent more, take a good look at what happened, and correct the problem for the next month.

There are two other things you should keep track of. The first is a record of your work. If you're going door-to-door, keep a record of how many doors you knock on, how many people answer, how many people want to buy what you're offering, and what time it is. That record will tell you how much success you're having compared to how much effort you're putting out. It will also help you know if you're going out at the wrong time of day—especially if a lot of people aren't home. Your work record will also help you know if you need to try some other sales approaches, if your present one isn't working.

If you're taking care of people's yards, keep track of what you did for each of your customers, and how long it took you. That will help you know if you're charging enough.

The final record you should keep is of your customers' names and addresses. Write down what you did for them (or what you sold them), the date, and the amount of money they paid you. As you build your customer list, you'll be able to learn which customers are giving you your most income.

INDEX

A

B

C

H

Habits, 55
Halloween insurance, 74-76
Halloween parties, 120
Handbill delivery, 151-153
Handicraft items, 53
Harvesting produce and fruit, 59-60
Hauling
  of broken branches, 70
  of junk, 69-71
Helping at parties, 23
Herb starts, 21
Hiring other kids, 25
Holiday parties, 120
Homemade bread, 65
Homemade cookies, 100
Honesty, 153
Hot pads, 50
Hourly rates, 24
Houseplant raising and selling, 159
Houses
  address installation on, 61-62
  cleaning of, 38, 114-116
  painting of, 23, 152
  watching of, 23, 138-140
Housesitting, 138-140
Hummingbirds, 40

I

Ice cream, 66
ID tags for pets, 84
Informality, 17
Inkodyes, 91
Insect spraying, 6
Installing street addresses, 61-62, 63-65
Instant cameras, 112
Insurance for Halloween, 74-76
Investors, 27, 136
Ironing designs onto T-shirts, 89-93

Is There Life After Housework?, 93, 115

J

Jobs
  odd, 23
  seasonal, 59, 68, 70, 107
  summertime, 68
  understanding of, 7
Junk hauling, 69-71

K

KIDCO, Inc., 26
Kids
  adult thinking about, 16
  craft sells for, 53
  framing service for art of, 155-157
  parties for, 118, 121
Kindling selling, 109-111
Kits
  Christmas tree stand, 126
  shoe-shine, 12

L

Ladders, 93
Laundromats
  bulletin boards in, 11, 24, 47, 69, 79, 115, 165
  taking care of clothes in, 102-104
Lawns
  care of, 140
  mowing of, 6, 23
  signs on, 47
  trimming of, 6
Leaflet delivery, 151-153
Leaf raking, 23
Letters of recommendation, 9
Library, 21, 41, 49, 58, 73, 90, 92, 115
Light bulb selling, 15-16
Liquitex, 91
Local gift shops, 53

shut-in, 168
Snow shoveling, 67-68, 140
Socket wrench set, 39
Soft drink selling, 17-18
Specialty shops, 173
Spraying for insects, 6
Spring cleaning, 114-117
Stamping machines, 84
Stamps, 45
Stands for Christmas trees,
    125-126
Stationery, 48
Stores as customers, 68, 108
Strawberry starts, 19-21
Street address installation, 61-
    62, 63-65
Stuffed toys, 57
Subscription service, 154
Summertime jobs, 68
Supermarket bulletin boards,
    11, 47, 69, 79, 115,
    165
Supplies, 36, 39, 137
Swap shows, 53
Swimming pool cleaning, 23,
    105-107

T

Table centerpieces, 38
Tags for pet ID, 84
Taking notes, 7
Taking orders, 31, 45, 57, 61,
    128
Tape selling, 15
Teaching, 10
Tools, 39
Toys, 57
Transportation, 44, 70, 83,
    136
Treasure maps, 143
Trimming lawns, 6
T-shirts
    advertising on, 47, 104, 150
    customizing of, 89-93
    selling of, 89-93
Tutoring, 10-11

V

Vacation-time home care,
    138-140
Vacuuming, 23
Valentine's Day parties, 120
Vegetables
    picking of, 59-60
    selling of, 160-162
Video tape players, 32

W

Wagons, 44, 83
Walking pets, 23, 54, 95-99
Washing
    cars, 23, 28, 37
    clothes in Laundromats,
        102-104
    dishes, 23
    dogs, 23, 98
    windows, 23, 93
Watching clothes in Laundro-
    mats, 102-104
Watching homes, 23
Water changing in cars, 39
Waxing cars, 37
Wholesale, 9, 15, 17, 31, 57,
    60, 92, 133, 146
Window washing, 23, 93
Word of mouth, 24, 48, 55,
    90, 165
Worm raising and selling, 11
Wrapping paper, 38, 127-129,
    135
Wreath making and selling,
    131-132
Wrenches, 39
Written agreements, 85

Y

Yard care, 6-9, 21
    equipment for, 8
Yellow Pages, 17, 31, 33, 87,
    91, 127, 133, 141

Extra Cash Books from Writer's Digest Books

Extra Cash for Kids, by Larry Belliston and Kurt Hanks. More than 100 ideas for kids age eight to sixteen who want to turn their spare time and vacation hours into extra cash—such ideas as tutoring others in backgammon or chess, growing and selling berry starts, cleaning airplanes, providing a newspaper clipping service, and selling Halloween insurance. Complete with details on how to do the job, set the prices, and avoid problems. 192 pages, $6.95.

Extra Cash for Women, by Susan Gillenwater and Virginia Dennis. Scores of home-based job ideas for women who want to turn their talents, creativity, and/or energy and enthusiasm into spare cash. The book contains information on how to do the job and tells what equipment is necessary, what pitfalls to avoid, and how to determine what to charge, plus business tips on advertising, recordkeeping, and raising start-up money. 312 pages, $8.95.

To order directly from the publisher, send the price of the book(s) (plus $1.50 postage and handling for the first book, 50¢ for each additional book) to:

Writer's Digest Books, Dept. B
9933 Alliance Road, Cincinnati, OH 45242

Prices subject to change without notice. Allow 30 days for delivery.